COMFORT ALL WHO MOURN

The Life Story of
Herbert and Madeline Nicholson

Written by
HERBERT V. NICHOLSON
and
MARGARET WILKE

Bookmates International, Inc.
Fresno, California

Comfort All Who Mourn

Published by Bookmates International, Incorporated. All rights reserved. Printed in the United States of America. No part of this book may be used or reproduced in any manner whatsoever without written permission except in the case of brief quotations embodied in critical articles and reviews.

For information write:

Bookmates International, Post Office Box 9883, Fresno, California, 93795, United States of America.

Typesetting and Production: MIC Innovative Creations, Lakeside, California.

Cover Design by: Colleen Dossey

Library of Congress Catalog Number: 81-71161

International Standard Book Number: 0-933082-05-3

The Lord has anointed me to bring good tidings to the afflicted. He has sent me to bind up the brokenhearted, to proclaim liberty to the captives, and the opening of the prison to those who are bound; . . . to comfort all who mourn.

Isaiah 61

To my beloved Madeline
who has indeed been a Spirit-filled
comforter to many

Contents

Illustrations

1. Ernie, Artie and Herbie, Rochester, New York 1894
2. Madeline, Cedar Rapids, two years old
3. Village evangelism
4. Grandma Nicholson and Virginia in rickshaw, 1924
5. Our home in Higashi Hara, 1931
6. At our front gate at Higashi Hara
7. Shimamura (left) and one night's guests at tramp lodge, Higashi Hara
8. Funeral at Manzanar Relocation Center
9. Virginia, Samuel and Donald with parents, 1949
10. Shimamura and his two children at old folks' home
11. Five condemned murderers at Sapporo with Nicholsons and officials
12. Relief goat leaving San Francisco
13. Presenting goats at Gotemba, 1948
14. Karuizawa home, 1961
15. Golden Wedding Anniversary, 1970

Foreword

I wish that I could remember exactly when and where I first met Herbert Nicholson. It seems I have known him all my life. But I know it was sometime during the chaotic and turbulent years of World War II. The memory is clearest about what he did at Manzanar War Relocation Center. There I saw him bring joy where there was sadness, hope where there was despair, and love where there was hate. He brought these gifts to us as we struggled for dignity behind barbed wire and watchtower.

There are those of us who remember him under the clear desert sky at another camp of Death Valley, California, where he sustained our hope and deepened our faith in God. And although I have seem him and Madeline, his extraordinary wife of 61 years, but a few times in the past three decades, I know that their influence is indeed forever.

When he asked me to write a foreword to his book, what could I say? How do you find the right words to acknowledge the gift of life? The pen cannot always write what the heart can feel.

The generation of Japanese Americans to which I belong now approaches the twilight years. We were teenagers and young adults when war drove us into the American version of the concentration camp. Thus it was at Manzanar and at some nine other detention centers across the land that we acquired our memories of wartime fears and bitterness, of courage and hope, of love and redemption. From the depths of those years when hope was slender indeed, when the entire globe was aflame with bloodshed and violence, the Nicholsons came into the desert to remind us of the healing power of faith and love.

Even today I remember wartime evacuation as a misguided act of American racism. Manzanar was the first of our wartime detention centers. And there our government initiated policies that ultimately were rejected. Manzanar had two standards—one for inmates, the other for overseers. We inmates lived in tarpaper barracks. Our overseers were provided finished bungalows. We received $12 to $19 a month for our work. They were paid ten to twenty times as much. We lined up to eat in mess halls. They were served in dining rooms.

Into this guarded camp came Herbert and Madeline Nicholson. He drove his stake truck. It was loaded time and again with everything under the sun that could get through inspection—all of it for us inmates. The Nicholsons ate in our mess halls, slept in our barracks, and with the sensitivity of saints, avoided identity with the privileged status of our overseers.

In 1963 the Pacific Southwest District Council of the Japanese American Citizens League presented a citation:

In Appreciation
Rev. Herbert V. Nicholson

For inspirational Christian love and lifelong unselfish dedicated service to improve and promote the welfare of persons of Japanese ancestry both in the United States and Japan.

I know something of what the Nicholsons continue to do each waking day—bringing comfort and good cheer to the sick and lonely. Lacking that depth, but striving for that faith which shines through in the lives of these wonderful people, I can only join with the multitude of friends and strangers whose lives have been touched by the Nicholsons, and we thank God for them, always.

Togo Tanaka
Los Angeles, California

Introduction

I have met Herbert and Madeline Nicholson in person only once. When it was first suggested in 1973 that I work with Herbert on his life story, I spent four memorable days in Pasadena discovering (and trying to keep up with!) these amazing people.

A spirit of hospitality pervaded the house at 1639 Locust Street. I woke each day to the chatter of birds under the eaves outside the front bedroom, and thought about the many guests the comfortable, old-fashioned room had sheltered over the years. Herbert was invariably up ahead of me and having devotions in his study before starting breakfast for us. The coddled eggs and toast were graced by sincere thanks for God's goodness and provision, followed by quiet reflection over the devotional readings in the *Daily Light* where the birthdates of family and friends were noted in the margins of the appropriate day's reading.

At the time of my stay Madeline was still able to get up a little, though she spent most of her time in a wheelchair due to great pain in her hip. Her memory was failing, especially about the present, but about the past she was clearer. If Herbert missed any words in the day's Scripture she was sure to notice. She knew the way to places frequently visited and reminded Herbert where to turn off the freeway whenever his avid talking while driving distracted him. Several times her quick, perceptive humor took me quite by surprise. On the fourth morning of my stay she looked at me a little puzzled and said with a warm smile, "I don't know where we got you, dear, but you are very welcome." Few words have touched me more.

The four days passed quickly, crammed with visits to

groups and friends, as well as a good number of scenic spots Herbert felt this Minnesota girl should see.

Although they were older, the Nicholson's life had not substantially changed from the life recorded in this book. It was all the same fabric, the same weave and texture as what had gone before—a life of simplicity, loving kindness, and plenty of action in behalf of others.

I am indebted to the editorial help I received from Mrs. Betty Mitson, a writer and researcher thoroughly familiar with both Japanese-American history and Mr. Nicholson's personal story. Her extensive notations on the manuscript were exacting, insightful, and often pointed and challenging. Any mistakes or misrepresentations that remain are my responsibility alone.

Margaret Wilke
New Brighton, Minnesota

Chapter 1

Pearl Harbor

"Sensei! Sensei!" Mr. Niwa was shouting and waving to get our attention as we drove by. I stopped, and as he ran up to us he gasped, "Sensei! They've bombed Pearl Harbor!" We could hardly believe our ears!

Worship services had ended at the West Los Angeles Japanese Methodist Church where I was pastor and my wife Sunday school superintendent. We had had our lunch and, as was our custom on Sunday afternoons, were on our way to visit congregation members when we were distracted by the frantic call from the sidewalk. The news brought immediate realization of the imminent dilemma our friends faced.

I had been pastor of this small church for a little less than a year when Japan's military might struck Pearl Harbor. Madeline and I had returned to the United States in 1940 after nearly twenty-five years of missionary service in Japan. Although we had been retired from our work there on behalf of the Society of Friends due to gathering war clouds, we did not feel we were "retired" from God's service. So, after getting settled with our family in Madeline's home town of

Pasadena, we began to look for work right where we were.

Just before Christmas 1940, Rev. Yuzuru Yamaka of the Los Angeles Japanese Methodist Church called to ask whether I would take the pastorate of a little church in West Los Angeles. I told him I could not possibly fill the post. I was a Quaker, not a Methodist, and could not really preach either in English or in Japanese. But Rev. Yamaka was not to be denied. Thus on the first Sunday of 1941 I found myself at the Sunday services of this little church.

About thirty Nisei (American-born Japanese) attended English-language services and about the same number of Issei (Japanese who had migrated to America) came to the Japanese services. I was just beginning to speak in Japanese that first Sunday when Rev. Yamaka came in and took a seat in the back of the room. In spite of my twenty-five years in Japan, my knees knocked together when I saw him because he was one of the finest Japanese preachers in California. But he smiled at me so encouragingly that I made it through the service.

After lunch the church members held a meeting and formally called me as their pastor. However, all the salary they could offer was half the salary of the regular pastor, Rev. Jun Fujimori, who was to have six months leave on half-salary due to ill health. As a Quaker I did not approve of a "paid" ministry, but I was willing to accept their offer of forty dollars a month, as it would little more than cover the car expense in driving back and forth to West Los Angeles from our home in Pasadena.

Thus began a wonderful Christian fellowship that prepared us for the unforeseen work we were to do during the war. As a pastor I was included in the Japanese Church Federation, and also in the Methodist Conference. I attended the meetings of both these organizations and became acquainted with many Japanese Christian leaders.

In July, Rev. and Mrs. Fujimori returned and took over

the Issei work, while I continued with the Nisei and Madeline with the Sunday School. She was S.S. Superintendent right from the start. We made lifelong friendships and had some deep spiritual experiences as we shared the love of God in both joy and sorrow.

I was the only Caucasian minister with an all-Japanese congregation at the time of Pearl Harbor. Later when the Evacuation came, my status was very important. All the Japanese pastors were taken away with the others, but I was left behind, by virtue of skin color only. I was free to do what I could for our people.

Now suddenly with the news of the Japanese attack we became part of the spreading waves of shock and disbelief that broke across the nation. We went back to the church at once where some of the members were still gathered. We phoned others and soon nearly everyone was present.

Many of the church members were gardeners. Rev. Fujimori and I knew that most would probably soon lose their jobs, so we told them they need not pay us our usual salaries. But they insisted! At Christmas two and a half weeks later they gave Madeline and me a hundred dollars! Those dear people kept on paying us even after they were taken to detention camps.

That evening we had supper with Mr. and Mrs. Gisuke Sakamoto, elderly members of the church. Mr. Sakamoto told us that he was on the FBI "blacklist" because he had been in the Japanese army as a young man during the Russo-Japanese War. All such veterans were under suspicion, and he felt sure he would be picked up that evening.

When we left for home we discovered that a blackout was in effect because it was feared the Japanese might attack the West Coast. After all, Pearl Harbor had been attacked only a few hours earlier. Because no lights were allowed, it took us two hours to drive the twenty-five miles back to Pasadena. When we reached home we were grieved to find that some of our elderly Japanese friends had already been taken into custody. Eighty-year-old Mr. Tsumataro Hiraiwa, who had been in the Sino-Japanese war in 1896, was one of these. The next morning we learned that the local police had also taken old Mr. Sakamoto, just as he had expected, and a number of other Japanese friends as well, to the Immigration Detention Center on Terminal Island in San Pedro Harbor.

Not long after our return from Japan in 1940, an FBI agent had called on us and asked if I would be interested in working for the government. They were looking for help from missionaries who knew the Japanese and could speak their language. As we talked I discovered that if I worked with the FBI I would not be allowed to live in California and could not be a friend of the Japanese, so I said at once that I could not possibly work under such conditions! Now, as I thought about what to do for the arrested Issei, I was glad for that previous contact.

The first thing I did on Monday morning, December 8, was to go to the FBI office in Los Angeles. The morning papers had been full of stories about sabotage supposedly committed by Japanese in Honolulu. I urged the FBI to put a notice in the papers that they had already picked up all the "potentially dangerous" Japanese, and that those who remained should be treated fairly. Otherwise, I felt that lies like the ones about the Hawaiian Japanese would soon be told about the Japanese in California. Nobody denied that the stories were false, but I was told that the FBI did not do publicity work like that!

Still determined, I went to see Commander Kenneth D. Ringle of Naval Intelligence, whom I had known when he was Naval Attache at the United States Embassy in Tokyo. I asked him to send out notices to the newspapers that all the dangerous Japanese had already been arrested and that the stories about the Honolulu Japanese were false. He regretfully told me that he was not permitted to do this, even though he agreed that most of the stories in the press were lies.

My next contact was the Los Angeles Federation of Churches. I was given permission to speak to their committee on the Japanese problem, which was to meet on Wednesday, and was allowed just five minutes to present my case. I urged the committee to do something about informing the public that the Japanese in our midst were not dangerous and should not be mistreated. I had spoken for only two or three minutes when the chairman of the committee rose in anger and shouted, "Stop! After what those skunks Kurusu and Nomura did in Washington, we can't trust any Jap!"

I left the room immediately, but waited outside to have a little talk with that "doctor of divinity." I realized that he was under great emotional strain, but I wanted to caution him against talking like that. When he came out I tried to get in a word with him, but he brushed past me without answering.

In the years ahead, we were to encounter this rejection of our pleas about the innocence of the American Japanese many times, especially in churches. When we asked for help in the various projects we undertook to aid the Japanese who were undergoing both injustice and hardship, we were often refused on the grounds that it would be "comforting the enemy"!

It was a position I simply could not understand. We knew that the Japanese in our midst were probably among the most loyal of any single group of people living in America. But because of their Japanese ancestry and heritage, they were being accused *en masse* on the basis of race alone. We KNEW they were not "the enemy," but our efforts to make this clear seemed to fall upon deaf ears.

Competitors of the Japanese, like nurserymen and farmers, and other anti-Japanese pressure groups were so active and the newspapers so inflammatory that most people, already emotionally upset by Pearl Harbor, turned strongly against the local Japanese. Everyone had his own personal story about Japanese with shotguns and shortwave radios. Even fair-minded people like Earl Warren, then California's Attorney General, testified that the state's immigrant and native-born Japanese represented a serious threat to American coastal regions. It is to his credit that before his death Warren wrote in his memoirs that he regretted the internment order against the Japanese and his part in it.

An organization called the Northern California Committee on Fair Play for Citizens and Aliens of Japanese Ancestry had already been organized several months before the Pearl Harbor crisis. Some famous people were members of this group, including Dr. Robert Gordon Sproul, president of the University of California and Dr. Robert Milliken of the California Institute of Technology. My wife and I joined this committee, but even they would take no steps to prevent the mass evacuation. Their reasoning was that they could not tell the Army what to do. To that we replied, "It's our Army, isn't it?"

Unable to get any other help, a handful of us, largely based in Pasadena, formed the Friends of the American Way. We were too small a group to turn the tide, but we did all we could to let the government and the public know how we felt about our loyal Japanese Americans.

Chapter 2

Japanese in America

At the time of the Pearl Harbor catastrophe most Americans, now suspiciously scrutinizing their Japanese American neighbors, did not realize that these Japanese already had a long history in American life. Most were not newcomers with deep ties to their mother country. Many now being interned had come to the United States long before I first went to Japan in 1915.

The first small groups of Japanese contract laborers came to Hawaii in 1868. Hawaii was at that time still an independent sovereignty. Sugar plantation owners, eager to find a supply of cheap labor, had exerted pressure on the Japanese government to allow workers to come to Hawaii under the contract system. Emigration at that time was illegal in Japan. However, a special agreement regarding small groups of contract workers was arranged. The experiences of those early Japanese in Hawaii were not good. Most returned to Japan when their contracts were up.

Then in the 1880's Japan experienced a population explosion. As a result, the Emperor removed the centuries-old law against emigration. Between 1890 and 1910, over seventy thousand Japanese left for Hawaii, with a few going on to California and the Northwest Territory.

Not long after the surge of emigration from Japan began, Hawaii applied for annexation to the United States. When it became clear that annexation was going to be accomplished, the plantation owners, concerned about their labor supply, stepped up their importation of Japanese contract laborers. Their object was to get them onto the islands before Hawaii became a U.S. territory and thus subject to American law. Of particular concern was the Labor Law Act of 1885 which prohibited the importation of Asian contract labor and nullified previous contracts.

Hawaii was annexed on June 14, 1900. This nullified the contract system. Thus released, many Japanese, about ten thousand a year, moved to the mainland where wages were slightly higher.

The timing of the arrival of the Japanese in California was unfortunate because it came just after what was considered the resolution of the so-called "Chinese problem." There had been considerable hostility toward Chinese immigrants because they had begun to rise as a group from the low manual labor jobs for which they had been brought to America, to a higher, more independent economic status. This was seen as a threat by white groups already in the occupations being entered by the Chinese. Eventually the hostility against the Chinese grew so strong that the government passed the Chinese Exclusion Act in 1882 which forbade any further immigration of Chinese into the United States.

Some of the anti-Chinese feeling transferred to the newly arriving Japanese immigrants. Like the Chinese, the Japanese came to the mainland to do the heavy manual labor that many whites refused to do—the work in the mines, fisheries, and canneries, in lumber mills and on the railroads. They were young, hard working, frugal, kept to themselves, and were willing to take low pay. On the whole, they were exactly what employers were looking for.

Many of the early Japanese had come to America hoping to make a lot of money, after which they would return to Japan. But as the years passed and fortune did not appear, many decided to stay longer. They began to think about wives and families. Until 1900 most of the Japanese immigrants to this country were unmarried men under thirty years of age. After 1900 women began to come from Japan, sent by parents or relatives to be brides for the Issei.

These women must be given considerable credit. They came alone to a new country to be married to a stranger, usually chosen for them by their families. It took tremendous courage. There must have been disappointments, but they stuck it out.

With families to think of now, many of the Japanese men became less and less satisfied to be ordinary laborers with no future. In Japan most of them had been farmers. Here in America they saw land, lots of land! Most of the Issei did not have enough money to buy their own land, so some agreed to a system of sharecropping to get started. Others rented or leased land from a landowner. A few were able to buy land, but very few were able to afford the good farm land, so they had to buy the land which nobody else would take, land considered useless for farming.

By grit and determination, the Issei made the wasteland bloom. They brought water where water was needed, and drained water where there was too much. They battled the elements and built up the soil until hundreds of thousands of acres of unimproved western lands were brought into cultivation. The land nobody wanted is now very valuable.

As early as 1905, a San Francisco newspaper ran the headline, "The Yellow Peril—How the Japanese Crowd Out the White People." Such articles claimed that the Japanese were trying to "take over" California. Racial arguments of an entirely unfounded basis were used to fan the flames of public prejudice.

In May of 1913 the California legislature passed the Alien Land Law which prohibited any alien not eligible for citizenship from owning land. Like all other Asian immigrants, the Japanese were denied the right to become naturalized citizens. They were therefore advised by lawyers to buy land in the names of their American-born children.

It is not surprising that the passage of this law brought an outcry from Japan. Washington tried to reassure Japan that these were purely local matters, not a form of racial antagonism fostered by the federal government. Though Japan accepted this explanation, the Alien Land Law had a permanently negative effect on U.S.-Japanese relations.

During the next ten years, every state where numbers of Japanese were living, with the exception of Utah, passed discriminatory land laws, including Delaware, Louisiana, and Missouri. Then in 1920, even the loophole of owning land in the names of minor American-born children was closed by the California legislature.

In spite of all this, and in some measure because they were not accepted into the mainstream of American life, Japanese communities began to develop. Like most immigrant groups, the Japanese tended to stick together where they could eat their own food and speak their own language. Japanese grocery stores, shoe repair shops, barber shops, hotels, and restaurants began to spring up in the cities on the West Coast, particularly in the older sections of the cities where the rent was cheap.

But living a separated life in this way can contribute to misunderstanding. As the Japanese became more firmly rooted in America, slowly rising on the economic scale to a more independent state, feelings of hostility against them began to grow in groups of jealous whites.

Being isolated, the Japanese were easy prey for special

interest groups that had something to gain by harassing them in the press. Since the greater mass of Americans had had very litle contact with the Japanese, it was difficult for them to recognize the clever lies for what they were.

In 1907 President Theodore Roosevelt and the Emperor of Japan entered into what is known as the Gentlemen's Agreement. It was an informal, extra-legal arrangement. Its terms, in brief, were that Japanese children in America under the age of sixteen would be admitted to public schools. In return, Japan would prevent emigration of most skilled and all unskilled laborers by refusing them passports. Families of Japanese already in America would still be allowed to emigrate.

Public feeling against the Japanese, however, continued to increase. In 1924 the government passed another exclusion law, the Immigration Quota Act of 1924, which cut off immigration of Japanese to America completely.

For the Issei who had carefully instilled in their children a love for America and loyalty to its government, the new law was a cruel blow because it said clearly at last, "Japanese not wanted here."

Chapter 3

"Potentially Dangerous"

Now again, almost twenty years after the Immigration Quota Act of 1924, governmental action against the Japanese was taking place. As soon as the reports of the attack on Pearl Harbor were confirmed, several hundred Japanese men and women were arrested as a "precautionary measure," in case they might be subversives working for the government of Japan.

Some six hundred "potentially dangerous" Japanese men from key areas along the Pacific coast were picked up within hours by local police and taken to various Department of Immigration Detention Centers. In the following days, a number of women were also arrested and interned in the Federal Building in Los Angeles. Even a few Nisei were taken into custody, such as Togo Tanaka, who had been the editor of the English section of the Los Angeles bilingual Japanese daily newspaper, *Rafu Shimpo*. He was detained for eleven days without being formally charged and then released without explanation.

I immediately began to do whatever I could to help. Monday afternoon I went to Terminal Island Prison, then the detention center for the Los Angeles area, to see some of my friends and report back to their families. I discovered that some two hundred of the men arrested were old men who had been in the Japanese army when they were young, before they had migrated to America. The others were leaders of the Japanese community or those who had entertained officers of Japanese battleships in training that had stopped at United States harbors before the war.

Fortunately I was allowed to see several of our closest friends, one at a time. I then visited their wives to report to them. Because the specific reasons for arresting Japanese were not known in the Japanese community, Issei men who had not yet been picked up lived in constant fear of arrest. In the midst of all the confusion and panic, I did all I could to help our many friends whose families had been torn apart and whose loyalty to America was suddenly being questioned. I was amazed at how quickly war can raise the ugly heads of suspicion and hatred in people who are normally generous and rational.

Not long after the first six hundred men were arrested, they were transported to Fort Missoula in Montana where the Justice Department was to conduct hearings in conjunction with the Federal Bureau of Investigation. The Friends' Service Committee asked me to continue my efforts on behalf of the Japanese families involved, on a larger scale.

My first responsibility was to drive to the Imperial Valley, a trip of several hundred miles, to visit other homes from which men had been arrested. Gurney and Elizabeth Binford, also missionaries to Japan, went with me. After our visits in the Imperial Valley, we drove to San Diego and then back to Los Angeles, stopping to comfort Japanese families wherever we could find them.

In January of 1942 two other Quaker men, Tom Bodine and Floyd Schmoe, accompanied me on a trip all the way up the Pacific coast to Seattle. Floyd and I then went by train over to Spokane, Washington, visiting homes of men who had been picked up, then on to Fort Missoula, Montana, where the six hundred men had been taken.

We arrived at Missoula on a Sunday morning. The head of the institution, Nick D. Collaer, kindly allowed us to go inside and hold a meeting with all the Issei. After the meeting was over we were allowed time to visit with the men, and I was able to talk with some of my personal friends without having to wait to see them one by one.

Later we visited at length with Mr. Collaer. He showed us some of the letters which the men in his charge had received from their families. All letters had to be in English and, of course, they were censored before being given to the prisoners. Collaer told me that, after reading the letters, he felt certain that these Japanese men were among the most loyal of Americans!

I was assigned to the "Nevada" hearings for fifty-two Japanese who had been arrested in Nevada where they had worked in a copper mine. For the next four days, I was interpreting from eight in the morning until ten at night. A gentleman from the Department of Justice conducted the hearings, with an FBI man acting as prosecutor. Three Nevada community leaders were present to decide the cases and there was a secretary to record the proceedings.

In each of the fifty-two hearings, the Department of Justice man asked the Issei why he was there. Of course, he didn't really know! The matter was not made any clearer to him when he was informed that it was because he was "potentially dangerous."

Each one was then asked questions such as, "What is your philosophy of life?" "What do you think of Pearl Harbor?" "If the Japanese army was landing on the coast of California, the American army was in the hills, and you stood on the beach with a gun, which way would you fire?"

Fifty of the fifty-two men were uneducated, *sake*-drinking laborers from the mine. They were not able to relate to the questions at all. It was finally revealed that the official reason they were arrested was that the foreman of the mine had taken fifty cents out of their pay each month to be sent to Japan for the relief of widows and orphans of soldiers who had been killed in war. When the men were asked why they had allowed this, most of them did not even know about it. The money had been deducted before they received their pay.

After four days of this absurd attempt at justice, the judges agreed that these men were not dangerous. They suggested that I go out and ask them what they would like to do: (1) go back to the mine; or (2) stay here at Fort Missoula. When I returned with the overwhelming decision of the men to stay, the judges roared with laughter. These poor laborers had never had such good food, comfortable sleeping quarters, or time for such amusement as card games on their hands. In spite of the unanimous decision of the judges that the men were innocent, half of them were sent to join their families at assembly centers and half were kept at Missoula as POWs to satisfy public opinion.

After the hearings were over, the men who had acted as "judges" told me they were grateful that I had given them a new "slant" on the American Japanese. As we boarded a train for home that night, I started toward the rear. They stopped me, saying that the sleeping cars were toward the front. I said I was riding coach.

Surprised, they asked, "Isn't Uncle Sam paying for your travel?"

"No," I replied. "All I got was this pencil the secretary gave me and a few free meals."

"Boy!" they exclaimed. "You worked harder than any of us!"

Public opinion was continually demanding that more "suspicious characters" be picked up by the police. So the government decided to apprehend all Buddhist priests and everyone who had taught in the Japanese language schools, all without a shred of evidence of any wrongdoing, held like criminals on suspicion alone! In the end, over 4,500 persons were arrested.

Since the government kept arresting so many "potentially dangerous" Japanese, it became impossible to keep them all in one place. The men arrested in Los Angeles were temporarily held in an old CCC (Civilian Conservation Corps) camp in Tuna Canyon just outside the city. This camp was big enough for about 300. When it was full, a trainload of men would be sent to one of the army forts in North Dakota, Montana, or New Mexico for hearings. After the hearings, they were usually either sent to relocation centers or kept in Army prisoner-of-war camps.

I made many visits to the Tuna camp and became good friends with the immigration official, Mr. M. H. Scott, who was in charge. Scott said to me one time, "I could tell these men to go home and come back tomorrow evening, and they would all be back on time. But in spite of that, we have to have a fence around them and place old Sarge at the gate with a gun!"

The women who were arrested in Los Angeles were kept in confinement there. I was a defense witness in several of the hearings for those who had been Japanese language schoolteachers. The hearings were held in the Federal Building in Los Angeles. The man from the Department of Justice who was in charge of the hearings was a large, rough-spoken man, extremely anti-Japanese. I especially remember his rudeness to little Mrs. Imamoto.

The man from the Justice Department had a Japanese textbook from which Mrs. Imamoto confirmed she had taught. He turned to a page which had pictures of a Japanese soldier and a flag of the rising sun on it and asked if she taught that page. Mrs. Imamoto replied that she replaced the flag in the picture with the Stars and Stripes and taught the children loyalty to America.

The official then asked which way she would shoot if she were standing between the Japanese army and the American army. She said she was a Christian and would not shoot either way. He continued his rude questioning until she began to cry.

When my turn came to speak, I said that Mrs. Imamoto's patriotism was way above his and that he should be ashamed of himself for making her cry!

The next day in the halls of the Federal Building I saw this same man coming toward me. I tried to avoid him, but when he saw me he came and took me by the arm, led me into his private office, and shut the door. I wondered what was coming!

He told me to take a seat. He wanted to talk. Then he surprised me by thanking me for what I had said about Mrs. Imamoto and assured me that she would be released at once. He asked me to tell him more about the Japanese. When I saw his changed attitude, I was glad to tell him all I knew.

Chapter 4

Quaker Education

My desire to help the American Japanese in their plight sprang from two sources. First, my many happy years as a missionary in Japan. And more importantly, it sprang from my heritage and commitment as a Quaker.

My ancestors left Sweden about 1600 A.D. because of military oppression and settled in the British Isles. My father, Arthur Lees Nicholson, was born in England on April 27, 1863. While he was still a young boy his family moved to Ireland. There he received a Quaker education at Newton Friends' School at Waterford in South Ireland.

When my father was twenty-one, he migrated to the United States and settled near Philadelphia. On Sundays he attended the meetings of the Society of Friends, and it was there that he met a lovely young woman, Margaret Fox Bentley. Margaret had also been born in England. It wasn't long before she and Arthur were deeply in love. They were married on May 17, 1888, in a simple Quaker ceremony.

My mother's middle name, Fox, is the same as the founder of Quakerism, George Fox, although she is not a descendant. The history of the Quakers is generally dated back to 1647 when, as a young man, George Fox came to a spiritual breakthrough after spending a long time fasting and reading his Bible as he wandered through Derbyshire, England. He recorded the event in his diary:

> . . . I heard a voice which said, "There is one, even Christ Jesus, that can speak to thy condition," and when I heard it my heart did leap for joy.

About 1660, under Fox's influence and teaching, the Religious Society of Friends came into existence. Among his followers there developed a distinctive style of worship. The discipline of silent worship was encouraged, stemming directly from Fox's own experience of Divine revelation.

Over the years Quakers have become well known for their belief in the equality of all men, an intensely practical commitment which has kept them in the forefront of social reform in many areas. In most Quaker groups there has also been an outspoken refusal to take part in war, combined with a determined effort to promote brotherhood among nations.

After my parents were married, they moved to Buffalo, New York where my brothers Ernest and Arthur were born. I was born on January 30, 1892, in Rochester, and Sidney was born two years later.

You can imagine what our household was like with four lively little boys under six years of age! I still have a slight scar on my forehead which was made when Ernie accidentally upset my high chair out of the living room window. I remember sitting in that same window crying as I watched my older brothers playing in the snow, wearing the boots they had received at Christmas. I was too little to have boots.

After Sidney was born we moved to Rahway, New Jersey, where my brother Leslie was born, and two years later a baby sister, Margaret, joined us. What joy, because we five little boys did want a sister!

In Rahway I began attending my first school, a one-room Friends' school. I was towheaded and fat, and being very bashful on the first day, I began to cry. The teacher asked Ernie to take me out of the room. He took me to the cloakroom and made me laugh by putting on girls' bonnets and making "Ernie faces."

At the turn of the century we moved again, this time to Media, Pennsylvania, a suburb of Philadelphia. Here a second sister, Sarah Eleanor, was born, making our family complete. Again we attended a one-room Friends' school. Although often we were called names by the public school boys across the street, I have many fond memories of those years and of our kind teacher, Rachael Wickersham.

All the pupils were members of the Society of Friends. Each week we were expected to memorize Scripture verses. On Thursday morning we recited them before attending the midweek meeting at 11 a.m. On my ninth birthday Mother gave me a leather covered Testament and Psalms. On the flyleaf she wrote in her beautiful hand:

> *Herbert Victor Nicholson, from his mother*
>
> *The Lord shall guide thee continually, and satisfy thy soul in drought; and thou shalt be like a watered garden, and like a spring of water, whose waters fail not. (Isa. 58:11)*
>
> *For the mountains shall depart and the hills be removed; but my kindness shall not depart from thee, neither shall the covenant of my peace be removed. (Isa. 54:10)*
>
> *He shall be victor over self and sin.*

I still have that little Testament. There are yellow marks at Psalm 103, which my dear Grandmother Bentley helped me learn. She was living with us at the time and would take me walking in the evening as we went over the verses together. I can still hear her sweet voice say, "Bless the Lord, oh my soul . . . ."

We moved again, settling finally in Lansdowne, Pennsylvania, where we lived until 1914. It was here that our roots grew deep in the Friends' school and meeting. Louisa Jacobs was our gifted Irish Quaker teacher, and an inspiration to several generations of Quaker children. She would take us on early morning bird walks, and discipline us in a way that did not irritate. I remember one incident very clearly.

My father was an architect and used very expensive pencils. When they got so short that he could not use them he gave them to us boys. I became tired of using such short pencils so was tempted one day when I saw a glass on Teacher Louisa's desk holding a whole lot of lovely, brand new pencils. At recess time when the children were out playing and the teacher had left the room, I took one of those pencils and put it in my pocket.

That day at the close of school the kind teacher looked very serious and said, "I had thirteen pencils in this glass and one is missing. I wonder who took it!"

I blushed and looked confused. She noticed it, of course, but she said, "All right, children, you may all be excused."

I thought to myself, "She said *all* and that includes me." But I know she must have noticed my confusion.

After everyone had left the room I went up to her desk holding out the pencil and crying. She put her arm about me and said, "Herbert, thanks for returning the pencil and promise me that thee will never steal again!"

Years later, when Teacher Louisa was ninety years old, she visited me when I was in the East. She told me that she had no memory of my having stolen the pencil, but she had once told her father a lie that had been on her conscience from childhood and was greatly worried about it. I told her that her father had died years ago and she could not tell him, but she could tell the Lord about it. So we had a little prayer right there, after which she said she felt so happy!

At home we were taught respect for discipline and order, for father firmly believed in it. On Saturday evenings everyone was expected to polish his shoes and get his clothes ready for Sunday. Sunday morning when we were all ready, father would set the pace and we marched in line, mother and the girls bringing up the rear, to the century-old stone meetinghouse about a mile away.

In the meetinghouse, father and we five boys sat on the men's side while mother and the girls sat on the women's side. We had to sit very quietly! Bearded Jacob Elfreth used to hold forth on his favorite texts, "Ye must be born again," and "The true worshippers shall worship the Father in spirit and in truth." Walter Haviland, a teacher, would give more intellectual messages.

I am grateful that we had to attend these solemn, un-programmed meetings, as, when I was twelve, God became real to me in one of them. It was a stormy day and one of the shutters on the old meetinghouse came loose and was banging. I suddenly realized that God was a force in the storm. From that day I have never doubted that there was a Creator God.

At home in the evenings father always read a chapter from the Bible. He was an excellent reader and made the passages interesting and exciting for us. After the reading, we would have a period of silence when mother sometimes would pray.

Mother was greatly interested in foreign missions. She once took us to a Presbyterian church to hear a missionary from China. He quoted Isaiah 6:8: "Here am I, send me." From that time, whenever I heard an appeal to become a missionary, I would say in my heart, "Here am I, send me."

After graduation at Lansdowne, we all went to Westtown Boarding School, which was noted for its "guarded religious education." Our mother had gone there years before. The 250 students and faculty were all members of the Religious Society of Friends. Life was simple, with nourishing food, plenty of outdoor exercise, and regular study with dedicated, well-trained teachers. Sunday was set aside for worship, letters home, afternoon walks, and an evening religious assembly. Thursday morning was given over to Bible study, memorization of Scripture and the midweek meeting. To make up for the time lost from our regular school work that day, we had school Saturday morning.

There were strict rules about dress and conduct. Only black, brown, or gray ties were allowed, and coat collars had to be cut so that there was no turnover, or lapel. Of course smoking, drinking, dancing, and card playing were taboo. No musical instruments were permitted, and boys were called down for whistling in the halls. However, when we were away on camp suppers we were allowed to sing popular songs. Having been brought up with discipline in the home, the Nicholson children tried to obey the rules.

I graduated from Westtown in 1909 and that same year entered Haverford College, also a Quaker school. During the summer I had worked on the farm of our much-loved "Aunt" Hannah Morris, a Quaker minister, and earned enough to pay for my first year at Haverford. The following three summers I chauffeured for Dr. Anna P. Sharpless in the Pocono Mountains. At the end of each summer, Dr. Sharpless would give me a check for $200. This, plus a scholarship I was granted, covered my expenses for the year.

Dr. Sharpless gave me plenty of sound advice and was a great influence on me. She did not approve of salaries paid for religious work, so she never contributed to the mission board. But when I later went to Japan as a missionary, she faithfully sent me a gift of $200. every Christmas, with which I was able to do a great deal of extra work.

At Haverford we had a student body of 150. There were only 35 in my class at graduation. The college had the distinction of having the highest endowment per student and the least number of students per professor of any college in the country at that time. It was a privilege to have such close association with those scholarly men. Professor Rufus Jones was especially loved by all. His messages at the midweek meeting, where attendance was required even for non-Quakers, made the occasion a welcome experience rather than a drudgery. While still in college, I signed a Student Volunteer card for missions after attending a conference in which the great missionaries Robert Speer and John R. Mott spoke. What giants of faith they were!

After graduation I was offered a job teaching at my old school at Westtown, and I temporarily accepted this position. I certainly was not a "born teacher"! I was glad that my younger brother and two sisters were students while I was teaching there because they were a great comfort to me when I was feeling discouraged.

In January of 1915 Billy Sunday came to Philadelphia for nine weeks of meetings. A large barracks had been built in a park in the center of the city. This was filled with people who came to hear him three times a day. Each Wednesday I had a half day off, so one Wednesday I went to the afternoon meeting. The place was so crowded that I had to stand in the rear. I've forgotten what Mr. Sunday's topic was, but at the end of the sermon he seemed to point straight at me and say, "You're a coward! You've always gone to church and considered yourself a Christian, but you have never once opened your mouth to confess Christ as your Savior." This really challenged me, and when he said, "If you're not afraid, come down and shake my hand," I "hit the sawdust trail," an expression which comes from the fact that the dirt aisles were scattered with sawdust. I shook his hand, thus publicly acknowledging my faith in Jesus Christ.

I went straight from that meeting to see the chairman of the Friends' mission board in Philadelphia, told him what had happened and that I was interested in missions. We talked about the possibility of my going to Japan to be secretary for Gilbert Bowles, one of the missionaries there.

I returned to hear Billy Sunday at the evening service. He preached on Romans 12:1: "Present your bodies a living sacrifice, holy, acceptable unto God, which is your reasonable service." I bowed my head and offered my body, mind, and soul to God in a way I had never done before.

The next morning was the day of our midweek meeting at school, and I told the whole student body what I had done. It was the first time I had ever spoken in a Friends' meeting. Several students afterward expressed a desire to hear Billy Sunday, so we made arrangements for them to go on Saturday. At the close of our regular Sunday meeting, after hearing Mr. Sunday the day before, 117 students rose to say they had accepted Christ as their Savior.

Not long after that, a member of the Friends' mission board invited me to have dinner with him so we could talk about Japan. At dinner he asked if I was willing to go to that particular field. I promised him an answer by the next morning. The next day was January 30, 1915, my twenty-third birthday. I told him I would go to Japan.

When the board member returned to his home in New Jersey, he told his friend Sherwood Eddy, a famous YMCA man, of my decision. Eddy was the speaker in a Quaker meeting that very night. During his talk he announced that Herbert Nicholson had just volunteered to go to Japan. A collection was taken and enough money was given to cover my fare to Japan and my first year's salary!

Not long after that, I heard how a woman had come up to Eddy after the meeting with tears in her eyes. She told him that Herbert was her son. She had been praying for me to go as a missionary for a long time, but I had known nothing at all about this prayer request.

Chapter 5

Off To Japan

I went to business college during the summer of 1915 to learn shorthand and typing, in preparation for being secretary to Gilbert Bowles who was a missionary in Tokyo. It was October before I actually left home. Mother was very brave as we said goodbye at the kitchen door. I walked alone through the woods to the trolley car, carrying my bag, with Spinner our dog at my heels. He saw me board the trolley and turned dejectedly home as it pulled away. Father met me at the Philadelphia station where I boarded the train.

It was a long trip across the country to San Francisco where I would take a ship to Japan. Relatives in California welcomed me and even took me to the 1915 San Francisco World's Fair before seeing me off on the tiny *Nippon Maru* of the Oriental Steamship Company.

Our little ship was an old Cunard liner. It had to have square-rigged sails to help the engines! Nevertheless, it got us safely to Japan. The captain was an Englishman, a better storyteller than navigator. The purser and doctor were Americans and the crew was Japanese.

We landed at Yokohama at 8 a.m. Thanksgiving Day, after eighteen rough days at sea. One of the Friends missionaries met me at the dock. Of course, everything was very strange. The clatter of wooden clogs, rickshaws, and many strange sights fascinated me. I was astonished at how crowded the electric train was that we boarded for Tokyo.

The most amazing thing of all happened after we arrived in Tokyo. A kimono-clad lady got up and offered me her seat on the streetcar! In Japan, women stand while men sit. But even the men give up their seats to children!

I felt it was most appropriate for my first meal in Japan to be Thanksgiving dinner. I had much to be thankful for. At last I was in Japan! The fifteen missionaries with the Philadelphia Society of Friends' Mission to Japan were present, so I met them all. Later that evening we all went to a restaurant for *sukiyaki*. The food was delicious, but having to sit on the floor, not knowing where to put my long legs, and having to eat with chopsticks, was quite an ordeal.

I lived with Gilbert and Minnie Bowles and their two sons on the Friends' girls' school compound. Just across the driveway from the Bowles' home was the teachers' residence. The first Saturday I went over to this building to get some information. No one answered the door, so I walked in and called out. A young lady I had not met before appeared at the top of the stairs. I must have looked embarrassed and she was not able to resist teasing such a greenhorn, so she said, "You needn't be afraid of me. I'm old enough to be your grandmother!" I soon learned that she was Madeline Waterhouse, an American Board missionary living at the teachers' residence while attending language school. One glance at her was enough to convince me that she was certainly no candidate for "grandmother"!

But I was too busy adjusting to my new environment to spend much time thinking about girls. My first job at the mission was to copy reports that had just been given at the annual mission meeting. I learned before long that I was not only to work for Gilbert Bowles, but for Horace Coleman and his wife as well. I had brought a dictaphone with me from America, and both Horace and his wife became skillful in its use. I wrote reams of letters for them, including very long ones to "Dear Mama," often containing intimate things very embarrassing to me.

Gilbert Bowles also spent hours dictating into my machine, only to find again and again that he had forgotten to turn the needle down so that nothing was recorded! Finally he resorted to writing on scraps of paper, since I could not take shorthand properly. Later he would hand me letters and ask me to answer them on my own.

In addition to my secretarial work for the mission, I held an English Bible class for students from the nearby universities. Once a month I went with Gilbert to the Japan Peace Society meetings. When I arrived in 1915, he was executive secretary of this organization, which was one of the first of its kind in Japan. Through these meetings, I came to know many influential Japanese, American, and British businessmen and missionaries.

Gilbert Bowles was a very humble man and very honest. Through this work he had an *entre* into the offices of many important Japanese. He also kept in close touch with the American Embassy and exerted a great influence on officials. He was indeed a "missionary statesman." But, he was first of all an ambassador of Jesus Christ. His main concern was always with the advancement of the kingdom through the conversion of individuals. After the Bowles family had visited in my parents' home while on furlough, my mother wrote me that she considered Gilbert Bowles one of the most Christ-like men she had ever met.

In the summer of 1917 when the Bowles went on furlough, I was left in charge of their house until the new missionary family arrived. I replaced Gilbert as executive secretary for the Japan Peace Society and also was secretary for the directors' meetings of the Japanese language school.

The night of September 30 there was a terrific hurricane and the compound was badly damaged. Cleaning up the mess was too big a job for our gardener alone. I had been unable to find any help until one morning when an American beachcomber appeared at the front door. He wanted some money for coffee. Two front teeth were missing and his dirty shirt was open, revealing an American eagle tattooed on his chest. I told him I never gave money for *sake*, but that if he wanted work, I could give him plenty.

He told me his name of *Sumisu* (Smith), his circus name, but that his real name was Ed Quick. He said his mother, Minnie Quick, lived in New York, but that he had not heard from her in years. I promised to pay for his board and room at a nearby inexpensive rooming-house, and to put aside money for his fare back to America. For about a month Ed had lunch with me daily and told me his story while he worked on the cleanup of the compound.

He hated school and had been absent so much that he had never learned to read or write. As a teenager he had joined a circus as the top man in a three-man act. Then, when the Spanish-American War broke out, he lied about his age, joined the army, and was sent to the Philippines. But he drank so heavily that he was soon given a dishonorable discharge and put aboard a transport ship for home. While the transport was in Nagasaki, Japan, Ed went ashore, got drunk, and missed the ship when it left. For eighteen miserable years he had been living in Japan, begging, stealing, lying, taking drugs, drinking, and living with women. When sober he worked for a small circus, but could never save up enough money to return home. Once, while in jail on some charge, he tried to take his life by cutting his throat with a broken beer bottle.

When our compound was cleaned up, I sent Ed to help repair the damage on another missionary compound, to keep earning funds for his voyage home. One day shortly

after Christmas, a letter arrived from Ed's mother, Mrs.
Quick. I went to his lodging only to find he was under the influence of drugs. The innkeeper promised to send him over
as soon as he was able. Just before New Year's Day he appeared at our back door.

We went into the study and I handed him the letter. His
hands were trembling so much that he could not open it,
and he handed it back to me to open. It contained a tintype
picture of his sister, Mabel, a dollar bill, and a pencil-written
letter:

> *Dear Ed:*
>
> *I was so happy to hear from you and I do want
> you to come home. I don't care whether you
> come in silk or rags. You are all I have because
> Mabel died on Thanksgiving Day. I am almost
> blind and a neighbor is writing this letter. Come
> home soon.*
>
>

Love,
Mother
>

Ed looked dazed and then fell to the floor crying, "God!
Why didn't you take me instead of Mabel? I'm just a good-
for-nothing sinner, and Mabel was a real help to Mother!"

I knelt beside him and told him to stop scolding God and
ask to be forgiven. He got up on his knees and prayed simply, "God, forgive me, a terrible sinner, and take me back to
Mother." He stopped trembling, and a bright look came into
his face. He stood up a new man.

At once I got him third-class passage on a Japanese
steamer for Seattle and wrote the Salvation Army there to
meet him. On January 9, 1918, I saw him sail, wearing a
decent suit with shirt and necktie and a most heavenly smile.
He kept bowing and repeating, *sayonara, sayonara* (goodbye).

I heard from Seattle that the Salvation Army had found

work for him and sent him on his way to New York. Soon a card came saying he was home, working in the daytime and threading needles in the evening for his mother, so that she could do sewing the next day.

In the summer of 1920 when my wife and I attended White's Bible School in New York, I wrote to Ed to see if it would be all right for us to visit him. A few days later at suppertime, we were told we had a visitor. It was Ed, dressed in neat overalls, with a cap in his hands, a grin on his face and two teeth still missing.

The next day we visited the large public school in the neighborhood where Ed was janitor. That night he had supper with us, dressed in a neat suit and looking fine. He told us that the quarry where he worked had closed down so he had found work in a dairy. But the depression kept getting worse, so he came to New York where he found his good job. Every week he sent money home to his mother. There was no doubt about it, Ed was keeping straight and a real miracle had happened in his life.

The year the Bowles were away was a difficult one for me, and one of intense searching on my part. I was becoming discouraged because there didn't seem to be any results in the lives of my Bible-study students. Also the war had spread to the United States, and the hope of world peace for which the Peace Society had been working seemed further away than ever.

Most of all, I was struggling within myself for a deeper spiritual life. I had promised to work with the Friends' mission for three years. The time would be up in late summer 1918, just one year away. I was not sure whether I should commit myself to another term of service, and even more important, I was not at all sure whether God had really called me to Japan at all.

On New Year's Day, 1918, I visited the home of one of the young men in my English Bible class. I found two other class members there with him. They looked embarrassed and told me they had been talking about quitting the Bible class. They did not think the Bible was helping them live a good life, and when "Christian" America became involved in the European war, they were certain Christianity had failed.

They were most surprised when I told them I had been thinking along the same lines. However, God had just shown me that Christ is still able to "save sinners," and I told them about Ed Quick and how God had changed his life. I was sure there was a God of love, and I urged them to join me in trying for just one more year to truly find Him. We shook hands and agreed to continue the search for one more year.

My close association with other missionaries through the board of the language school often stimulated my thinking. We frequently discussed personal problems, and our ideals and values. Once we discussed what we would do if a robber entered our home at night. As a pacifist I felt that I would try to be kind and understand the man, and, if possible, give him what he wanted. One young missionary was especially outspoken about this issue. He said he would fight before he would let anyone take his money!

One day the following summer at Karuizawa, the lovely mountain rest area for missionaries on vacation, this young man withdrew thirty yen (about $15.00) from the bank. A Japanese carpenter saw him do it and followed him home.

During the night the carpenter entered the cottage armed with a knife. The young missionary was stabbed. I think he must have tried to stop the intruder. The wife joined in the fight and she, too, was seriously wounded. The carpenter found the $15.00 and fled, leaving the victims bleeding on the floor. By morning they were both dead. They lost their lives for only $15.00! You can imagine what an impression this tragedy made on my pacifist convictions!

That winter the "Oxford Group" headed by Frank Buchman came to Tokyo. They held small group meetings with times of listening and sharing. Although I found them helpful, they failed to take me to the spiritual depths for which I was longing.

But the next summer John Paul of Asbury College was at Karuizawa for the "Deepening of the Spiritual Life Conference." He was a godly man and touched the heart of my condition. He helped me to understand the meaning of the second coming of Christ and yet was sympathetic with my Quaker pacifist views. Paget Wilkes of the Japan Evangelistic Band, a spiritual holiness group from England, was also at our conference in Karuizawa. Paget was well-educated, a member of the Church of England and greatly used in conferences and private interviews. He was a man with a glowing face, and was truly "ablaze for God." The influence of these godly men began to lead me into the Baptism of the Holy Spirit for which I was earnestly seeking.

On September 9, Paget Wilkes invited me to have supper with him. After supper we talked, read the Bible, and prayed. At ten o'clock this dear man said to me, "Herbert, there is nothing more I can do for you, so I'll leave you in God's hands." He went upstairs and, as I learned later, knelt by his bed until midnight when he had a wonderful sense of victory for me, and only then got into bed.

I continued in prayer and meditation until midnight. Then I happened to look up and noticed for the first time a framed Scripture text hanging on the wall: "The God in whose hand thy breath is, and whose are all thy ways, hast thou not glorified." (Daniel 5:23)

In a flash I realized what the trouble was. When I had "hit the sawdust trail" it had not been as a penitent sinner, but rather because I had wanted to prove that I was not a coward. At the time that I had dedicated myself to God I had held on to my own good works, expecting to get credit for them. I had never been convicted of sin and come to God through the atoning power of Jesus Christ on the Cross. But now, like Ed Quick a few months earlier, I fell to my knees and cried to God, "Be merciful to me, a sinner. Forgive me, in Jesus' name."

In that moment God's great love swept over me. He cleansed my heart and filled it with His Holy Spirit. I rose to my feet, a "new creation," filled with God's treasure—His Holy LOVE. And, now that I had found what my heart had been searching for, it was also clear to me that God wanted me to give my life for service in Japan.

Chapter 6

The Captain's Daughter

In those days travel by train and ship took a lot of time and was expensive. Single missionaries usually went to Japan for five years their first term, and for seven-year terms after that. Married missionaries had seven-year terms from the start. When I originally volunteered to go to Japan, I volunteered for only three years because I was not sure God was calling me there. As soon as it became clear to me in the fall of 1918 that the Lord wanted me to remain in Japan, I agreed to stay two more years.

The mission advised me to attend language school. In three years I had picked up considerable Japanese, especially during the time I had lived with the Ishizukas, a family that spoke no English. Because I was entirely self-taught, my Japanese was not always very clear. Fortunately the Ishizukas' young daughter Michan could understand me. She would go with me when I went shopping to interpret my queer Japanese to the shopkeepers.

I was allowed to enter the second year at the language school, in spite of the fact that the head teacher pronounced my Japanese to be *shikataga nai*, meaning "it can't be helped." His opinion was not much improved by the time I graduated. Although I went to school five mornings a week, I also did full time work for the mission in the afternoons and evenings, so I really had no time for serious study.

I felt I had a clear call for rural evangelism, and began to spend my weekends in Ibaraki Ken, a rural province just north of Tokyo. Each Saturday I went to the home of one of the Japanese families in the countryside, and then on Sunday morning went into the town of Tsuchiura for an English Bible class and the Friends' meeting for worship.

The following summer, 1919, I did some camping, spending several weeks in the mountains with Japanese students and with boy scouts from the American School, as I had done in previous summers. And, of course, I attended the "Deepening of the Spiritual Life" conference again at beautiful Karuizawa. This time I noticed that Madeline Waterhouse was also a regular attender.

Madeline was known to everyone as the *imooto* or "little sister" of the Omi Brotherhood, a mission which had been founded by Merrell Vories in the Omi district near Kyoto. As a young man Merrell had come to Japan through the help of the International YMCA to teach English. In his first year at a commercial high school in the town of Hachiman, he won over forty young men to Christ. This alarmed the local priests and they arranged to have him fired. But instead of going back to America, he remained in the area and started the Omi Mission, which later changed its name to the Omi Brotherhood.

Madeline's older brother, Paul Waterhouse, a graduate of Princeton, had also come to Japan to teach English, helped by the International YMCA. He was teaching at Waseda University when he met Merrell. They became good friends. When Paul's two-year teaching contract ended, Merrell invited him to join his mission. Paul decided to return home first, to attend seminary and prepare for such work. He enrolled in Hartford Seminary in Connecticut where he met and married Bessie Peake. They returned to Japan in 1912.

Madeline, too, wanted to go to Japan as a missionary. Even as a girl at Pomona prep school in California, she had been a student missionary volunteer. She went to Oberlin College in Ohio for two years, and then transferred to Hartford Seminary's School of Religious Pedagogy because Paul felt it would better prepare her for mission work.

In the spring of 1914, she became ill and had to quit school. That summer, after recovering, she had an opportunity to travel to Japan with Merrell's parents. "Pop" Vories, as he was known to everyone, was going to Japan to help Merrell as treasurer of the commercial work the mission was doing. Madeline's father, Captain Waterhouse, felt the trip would be good for his daughter, so he gave his approval. Madeline's "visit" became a call to give her life to Japan. She returned to Hartford and graduated in the Spring of 1915. She arrived in Japan that September to begin her first five-year missionary term.

I also arrived in Japan in 1915. I met Madeline during my first years there, but I never gave her much thought because I wasn't really interested in girls. I was a close friend of Merrell and of her brother Paul, so I often saw her, although I never thought of her as anything other than "little sister."

Then in 1919, an incident occurred that really made an impression on me. Merrell got married. His bride was a lady from a noble Japanese family, so the wedding was quite an elaborate affair. I was to be the head usher at the wedding. Another young man and I, all decked out in frock coats and grey gloves, were to lead the wedding procession down the aisle.

Madeline sang a solo, a poem Merrell had written set to the tune of "Consolation." She was wearing a beautiful new dress of pink *crepe de Chine*. The wedding guests were numerous. Everyone wanted to be there because the daughter of this famous family was marrying a foreigner!

The reception afterward was held at a beautiful home in Tokyo. I was eating ice cream, and somehow, I managed to spill some of it on Madeline's new dress! I was horrified, but she didn't get mad at me! This made such an impression on me that I began to take serious note of her for the first time.

So during that summer of 1919 when I discovered that Madeline was also attending the spiritual life conference at Karuizawa, I decided to start visiting her. She was staying at a cottage belonging to the Omi Brotherhood. Her brother Paul and his wife Bessie were on furlough that year, which turned out to be a good thing for me, as she was lonesome for company.

On Saturday, September 6, I called on her at the cottage and found her dressed in a pink "Mother Hubbard" apron, doing the laundry. She finished her work and we began talking about spiritual things. She told me that she had also recently received the gift of the Holy Spirit.

Before we knew it, "Pop" Vories called from the next cottage, "Madeline, it's time for lunch."

"I have a visitor," she called back.

"Bring him along," Pop said, and she did.

After lunch was over and I had left, Mother Vories remarked, "He's so young, Madeline!"

On Monday I again visited her at the cottage and blunderingly said something about the possibility of marriage! She replied candidly, "If you're not sure about it, you had better spend a day in the mountains to find out what God really wants."

The next morning, September 9, exactly one year after my spiritual experience in Tokyo, I climbed to Sunset Point for a day of prayer and fasting. I found a sheltered place by a large tree and sat there all day praying, reading my Bible, and meditating. Finally, I opened my Bible at random and read these words from Isaiah 61:

The Spirit of the Lord is upon me; because the Lord has anointed me to preach good tidings unto the meek; he has sent me to bind up the brokenhearted, to proclaim liberty to the captives, and the opening of the prison to those who are bound — to comfort all that mourn — to give beauty for ashes, the oil of joy for mourning, the garment of praise for the spirit of heaviness, that He might be glorified.

These words came to me as a definite call to God's service. It also seemed clear to me that Madeline was to share the work with me. I went down the mountain straight to her cottage and very definitely and urgently proposed. How happy I was when she accepted!

Madeline was a Congregationalist. Her great-grandfather, the Reverend John Waterhouse, spent 29 years as a successful Methodist preacher and administrator in England, and then was appointed "Superintendent of the Missions in New South Wales, Van Diemen's Land (now Tasmania), New Zealand, and the Islands of the South Seas." He spent three strenuous years traveling from island to island and was welcomed everywhere with enthusiasm. Throngs came to listen to his powerful preaching. His administration was so successful that the work grew everywhere. However, often exposed to the elements, he was greatly weakened, and died at the end of these three sacrificial years.

His eldest son, John Thomas, settled in Tasmania, but because the climate caused health problems for him also, he moved to Hawaii on the advice of his doctor. Thus Madeline's father, Willie, John's youngest child, was born in Honolulu and grew up there.

As a small boy Willie loved to play on the beach and became well acquainted with the fishermen of King Kamehameha V, often going fishing with them. One day while watching them wash their nets, he saw some other rough fishermen come who began to molest the king's men. Young as he was, he took it upon himself to reprove these scoundrels, threatening to report them to the king. When King Kamehameha heard of Willie's bravery, he called for the boy to appear before him, and presented him with a fine canoe. Later a messenger was sent to tell Willie's father that since the king had no male heir, he wanted to adopt Willie! Of course Willie's parents did not agree to the king's proposal.

Madeline's mother, Milicent Philena Smith, was born in Hawaii, too. Her parents were medical missionaries, Dr. and Mrs. James William Smith. Willie and Lena met in school in Honolulu and were married in 1876. Then they moved to Cedar Rapids, Iowa, where eight of their ten children were born, including Madeline. In 1895, they moved to Pasadena.

On arrival in Pasadena the family left the train at Lake Avenue and walked a block north to Villa Street where Father Waterhouse had purchased a large English-type home. Their new home was on the outskirts of the city where there was no church, although a Sunday school had been started in a horsecar barn nearby. Father Waterhouse bought a lot at Lake and Maple, and with the neighbors built a small building for their Sunday school. In November of 1896 a church was organized, and joined the Congregational denomination. The Lake Avenue Congregational Church of Pasadena today is a large, flourishing congregation which has supported hundreds of missionaries through the years, including Madeline, who was the first member missionary they commissioned.

Only a day or so after she had agreed to marry me, I saw Madeline off to Kyoto where she would be teaching at the Doshisha Girls' School, a large university run by the Congregationalists and founded by the famous Christian educator Niijima. Then I returned to Tokyo. In the days and weeks that followed, letters from Kyoto to Tokyo and back flowed freely. But one day I received a letter in which Madeline expressed doubts about our engagement. We hardly knew each other, she said. Besides, we belonged to different denominations, and to top it all, she was four years older than I.

My good friend Paget Wilkes happened to be in Tokyo at the time and I shared the letter with him. He was so concerned that he invited us both to visit him in Kobe and talk it out. Early in October we met at his home. He left us alone in a quiet room while he went aside to pray.

When it was nearly time for Madeline to return to Kyoto, he knocked at the door. When he came in, he found us still sitting in opposite corners of the room! Since he and I were scheduled to attend an evangelistic crusade in another community that afternoon, he suggested that Madeline think things over some more and send a telegram if she wanted me to stop and see her in Kyoto on my way back to Tokyo. She agreed to that arrangement.

The famous evangelist R. A. Torrey was the speaker for the meeting Paget and I attended. A good friend of mine, Mr. Kurumata, was his interpreter. That night after the service, which had been held in a large tent, Paget and I were housed in the home of some missionaries where Dr. and Mrs. Torrey were also staying.

Since there were only paper sliding doors between our room and the room where the Torreys were staying, and one of them was very hard of hearing, we could hear everything they said.

"That interpreter was terrible!" we overheard Dr. Torrey say to his wife. "I would say a simple sentence like, 'As in the days of Noah,' and he would take five minutes to interpret it!"

Dr. Torrey did not realize, of course, that the audience

had never heard of Noah, so Mr. Kurumata had to tell the whole story of the flood!

The next morning Paget and I were up early. He was kneeling on one side of our bed with his Bible open before him while I was on the other. With his ruddy face glowing he exclaimed, "Herbert, isn't it wonderful! You're a young man and I am much older. You're an American and I'm an Englishman. You're a Quaker and I'm a member of the Church of England. And yet we are one in Christ!"

Just then there was a noise at the entrance and we heard someone call *"Dempo! Dempo!"* (telegram). Paget beat me to the door and opened the telegram.

"She says come!" he shouted. "Hurry! Be off to the train."

Madeline was given the day off so that we would have plenty of time together, and we confirmed our engagement on that day, October 9. That night we went for a walk in the lovely grounds of the palace where the Emperor used to live, which is now a public park. It was a moonlit night and it was wonderful to see Madeline's face looking up at me with the moon shining on it. Time passed all too quickly, and I had to return to my work in Tokyo while Madeline went back to her teaching.

During Christmas vacation in 1919, Madeline came to Tokyo to be with me for the holidays. I was eager to show her around and share my dreams of working in rural evangelism. I took her first to Tsuchiura where we met all the people and talked about the time we would come to work there. We even looked at a piece of land we might buy. Then we went on to Mito and spent New Year's there. Madeline stayed with Edith Sharpless, a single Quaker missionary, and I with Gurney and Elizabeth Binford. We got up early on New Year's morning and went out together to Tokiwa Park to watch the sun rise on the year that was to mean so much to us—1920.

Of course we had written our parents about the engagement. Both families were delighted. Since we were due for a furlough, our first thought was to wait and be married at home in the United States. However, there was a great need for a teacher at the Friends' Girls' School in Tokyo for the spring term, and Madeline was asked if she would be willing to fill the position. She felt she should accept, so we planned to be married during spring vacation.

Our wedding was planned for March 31. A delegation from the Friends' mission board was in Japan at the time, so they were all present for the occasion. Walter Haviland, a close friend of my family and the chairman of the missions board, traveled with me by train from Tokyo to Kyoto.

Miss Denton, head of the foreign teachers' residence at the Girls' School and College connected with the Doshisha, met us at the station with a rickshaw. She was a remarkable woman, completely dedicated to the work at great sacrifice to herself. When we arrived at the house, Madeline met us at the door looking lovely.

That night Walter and I slept in a double bed with a charcoal brazier to keep us warm. In the morning Miss Denton came to our door and called out, "Mr. Haviland, will you have tea or coffee?"

Her voice was so commanding that Walter replied, "Coffee," although he really took neither!

After breakfast Madeline and I went to the Kyoto city office in the rain to change her name from Waterhouse to Nicholson and to inform them of her change of address. This was all that was necessary to make the marriage legal in Japan. American citizens were expected to go to the American Consulate for an official ceremony as well, but since the vice-consul had agreed to attend our wedding personally, this was not necessary.

It was still pouring down rain at three when the guests gathered for the simple Quaker ceremony. Appropriate music was played on the piano. Madeline and I simply walked forward and took seats on the front row.

After a pause, we rose and held right hands. Facing my bride I said, "In the presence of God and these, our friends, I take thee, Madeline Clara Waterhouse, to be my wedded wife, pomising with Divine assistance to be to thee a faithful and loving husband, as long as we two shall live."

Then, with appropriate changes, Madeline said the same thing to me. A certificate in Friendly fashion had been drawn up, so before them all we signed our names. Walter Haviland had previously explained to the guests the manner of a Quaker wedding, and after we exchanged our vows he gave a short message. Our dear friend Paget Wilkes also spoke briefly.

After the service the guests signed the marriage certificate as witnesses, and we went into the dining room where the Japanese staff had prepared delicious refreshments. The following morning Madeline and I left for a two-day honeymoon at her brother Paul's home on our way to Tokyo. Paul and Bessie were on furlough in America.

Back in 1905 Madeline's father had once run for mayor of Pasadena, and to the amazement of the family he was elected! Since he had a seagoing yacht, the community always referred to him as "Captain Waterhouse." My own father had spent a brief career as cook on a seagoing vessel before migrating to the United States. So you see, the son of a sea cook married the captain's daughter!

Chapter 7

Riding the Rails

Madeline and I settled in Tokyo in a tiny upstairs room in the home of my friends, the Ishizukas. We had to climb a steep stairway to get to our room and pass through the room where Mr. Ishizuka did his writing. He was a Japan Bible Society colporteur who often took trips into the countryside with a handcart loaded with Bibles and tracts, distributing them as he went.

During the winter Mr. Ishizuka spent his days writing tiny Japanese characters. It was his dream to write the whole Bible on one sheet of paper so that one could see all the promises of God at one glance. But since he felt it was not right to copy the Bible without preparation, he first wrote a thousand-character Chinese proverb *(Senji-Mon)* a thousand times, on a sheet of paper three feet by six. This meant that each one thousand characters would take a little over one square inch! With a magnifying glass and a three-haired brush, he patiently did this writing day after day. It took him four years, 1914-1918, the years of World War I, to complete this preliminary task.

Then he wrote the same thousand-character Chinese proverb once with a large brush on a sheet three feet by six.

He mounted both sheets, placed them carefully in a box, borrowed a frock coat and carried them to the palace to present to the Crown Prince (the present Emperor Hirohito).

Now at last Mr. Ishizuka felt ready to begin on the Bible, which would be about the same number of characters. When he finished, after much painstaking labor, he mounted it and used it to show at churches. It was greatly admired by the Japanese. The British Museum offered him a good price for it, but he refused their offer and presented it to the Japan Bible Society instead. He then kept busy writing the New Testament or certain books, for which the Japanese paid him well. In my Bible I have the Sermon on the Mount written by him in this way.

Each morning we had breakfast with the Ishizukas, their small daughter Michan, and two high school students. Mr. Ishizuka always read the Bible and prayed before the meal. One morning he read Psalm 127 about children being "an heritage of the Lord," and "happy is the man who has his quiver full of them." Then to my great embarrassment he prayed loudly that we might soon be blessed with children.

Madeline enjoyed teaching at the girls' school that spring and was especially pleased when she was asked to teach a Bible class in Japanese. By this time she had been in Japan five years and her Japanese was excellent. The spring term passed quickly, and in the summer of 1920 we were ready to take our first furlough home.

We sailed in July on the *Persia Maru* for Hawaii. We had a nice outside cabin to ourselves. Madeline was a bit sick at first, but soon was fine and we had a very happy voyage.

We stopped first in Honolulu to visit Madeline's many relatives. Her Uncle Will Smith met us at the wharf, and we soon found ourselves in their lovely home where Aunt Minnie was a wonderful hostess. Uncle Will was full of fun and introduced me to all the aunts, uncles, and cousins as "Mr. Madeline Waterhouse." Then we took an inter-island steamer to Kauai where Madeline's parents were staying with her oldest brother, Dr. Herbert Waterhouse. It was great the way they took me into their hearts at once as a son.

One day Father Waterhouse took me aside and said, "Don't tell Madeline, but I have a very weak heart and may pass on at any time." He was not yet 70, but lived to be 91!

After two wonderful weeks, we boarded the *Korea Maru* for San Francisco. It was so crowded that Madeline and I had to have separate rooms. One of her roommates was a woman of questionable character with frequent men visitors during the night, so Madeline preferred to sleep on a deck chair just outside my porthole, with a string tied to my finger for safety. I got up at four every morning, before the crew came to wash down the decks, to help her get back to her room.

We landed safely, and after a month visiting all the relatives in Pasadena, we took the Santa Fe train east to visit my family. My farmer brothers met us at the Woodbury station. Father and Mother welcomed us at home, as did our dog Spinner. At first Spinner was not at all friendly to Madeline, but later when I had to take a trip to Canada, Madeline and Spinner walked together through the woods to see me off on the streetcar, and from that time on he was always close at her side.

In the year before I had left for Japan, my brothers had bought a terribly run-down farm, which we had named "Echo Farm." It took years of hard work to make the farm prosper, but even before that time it was a happy place, with the latch-string always out for visitors. Through the years many Japanese, as well as missionaries, have been welcomed there as guests.

The Friends' meeting where my family attended accepted Madeline as a full member, even though she was a Congregationalist. On our brief visit to Pasadena earlier, Madeline had offered to resign from the Lake Avenue

Church, anticipating that she would join my meeting, but they would not accept her resignation. They just took me in too! So we enjoyed a dual membership. We did a lot of deputation work, raising funds for the Friends' mission board and for the new mission work we hoped to begin at Tsuchiura on our return to Japan.

As the time drew near for us to return to Japan in the fall of 1921, Madeline was expecting our first baby, so the mission board allowed us to remain in the States until after the baby was born. Madeline went to the hospital on Sunday morning, November 20, and at 11:15 that night Virginia gave her first cry. What a joy it was to have a daughter! I wrote in my *Daily Light,* "Virginia, 8 pounds, 11 ounces, miracle from God."

We returned to Japan in March, 1922, on a wreck of a steamer that was scrapped soon after the voyage. Madeline was sick for several days, so I had full charge of the baby until Madeline got her sea legs.

When we arrived in Japan, we found we were not to go to Tsuchiura as we had hoped. While we were away trouble had developed in Mito and the Binfords felt they should leave and start a new work in Shimotsuma. That left an empty missionary residence in Mito. So we were asked to take over the work there.

Instead of building a new home, we found ourselves moving into a 150-year old house just across the street from the Mito meeting house. We were given permission to use some of the money we had raised on furlough to modernize the old Japanese home. We covered the open well with its unsanitary moss-covered oak buckets and installed a force pump to run water into a tank high enough to have running water upstairs, as well as in the kitchen. Then I took a corner out of an upstairs bedroom to put in a bath and flush toilet. This was the first flush toilet in Ibaraki Ken.

Madeline was kept busy at home with the baby and many

visitors. She also did what she could to help with womens' work and Sunday school. I continued teaching the English Bible Class that Gurney Binford had started, and worked closely wth the pastor of the Mito meeting, who lived with his family in an old thatch-roofed cottage behind the meeting house. In addition, I was advisor for a small dormitory of junior college students and taught English conversation classes in the local high schools four mornings a week.

There were many things to be learned about living in a Japanese town. For example, there were some valuable pine trees in our garden that needed trimming twice a year. The first time we hired a gardener he seemed unusually deliberate. Through the windows we could see him squat down on his haunches and look intently at the tree while filling his small pipe with tobacco. He would light the pipe, take three puffs, knock it out on a stone, fill it again, and then light it by picking up the still-burning first pinch. Then, three more puffs and he would repeat the operation. Finally, he would slowly rise and continue to trim the tree.

At about ten o'clock we served him the customary tea and cakes, which took more time. At noon, while he was slowly eating his lunch, I couldn't stand it any longer and told him that I was paying him to work, and he was spending as much time sitting as working. The man became quite indignant and told me he was not doing the job for money, but to see to it that it was done in the way it ought to be. What a reprimand to the missionary that was!

An elderly doctor lived across the street from us, but refused to ever send us a bill for his services. We had been told that it was not customary for doctors to present bills, but that we should give him a good present at New Year's. So we asked a fruit store to take a large box of apples, greatly prized in Japan, and deliver it to this doctor's house as a gift on New Year's Day.

When the gift arrived, the doctor rushed over to our house in his slippers, quite upset because he didn't want us to give him anything! An hour later his maid appeared in her best kimono carrying a tray covered with a silk scarf. It was his return gift! We never were able to "get even" with this kind doctor.

Each year in the heat of the summer we went to Karuizawa for a time of refreshing. In the summer of 1922, we bought a piece of land from the Omi Brotherhood and had them build a cottage for us. This became our summer home and we never tired of the beauty of the place—the murmuring stream, singing birds, lovely cool woods, and our delightful missionary neighbors.

During our second summer at Karuizawa, we experienced one of Japan's historic events, the disastrous earthquake of September 1, 1923. I was in a committee meeting when the earthquake began. The building shook as if it would collapse at any moment. As we all ran out, I saw Madeline coming to meet me from shopping. We rushed toward our cottage with buildings, trees, telegraph poles, and everything else shaking and swaying all around us.

Virginia was asleep in our cottage with a reliable Japanese woman in charge. We were relieved to find that she had not even awakened. The Japanese woman had wisely taken the charcoal fire out of the kitchen at the first sign of the earthquake. The cottage stood firm and we were grateful.

By evening we could see the glow from the hundreds of fires in Tokyo. The whole city was burning! The next morning, Sunday, there was no news at all since the wires were down, but rumors of the catastrophe were flying everywhere. We were concerned about our friends at the Tokyo Mission and at the Friends' Girls' School. Gurney Binford of our mission and I decided to go to Tokyo on Sunday afternoon on his motorcycle to check on the damage.

We reached the suburbs of the city at nightfall and

camped in a temple yard until daybreak, when we started out again. The streets were crowded with refugees. Some of the buildings in the city were still burning. It was a terrible sight. When we arrived at the compound of the Girls' School we found the buildings badly damaged, but were relieved to find that the fire had stopped at the fence of the compound. We spent the rest of the day going around to find our friends and do all we could to help.

That night Gurney took me to the train station on his motorcycle so I could return to Karuizawa with the news. Unfortunately, a bridge was out so no trains were running from Tokyo. At the first station outside of Tokyo there were so many people crowded around that we could not even get near the place, so Gurney took me to the next station where only a few people were waiting and left me there.

I stood on the platform and waited. When a train finally came, it was unbelievably crowded, with people on the roofs, in the coal car, and even on the engine. It looked hopeless for me to find a place, but having long arms and legs, I was able to get my feet on a step, grab the hand rails and eventually squeeze my way onto the coal car.

At every station there were crowds of people waiting. At one station the crowd discovered a Korean and threw him off the train, beating him with bottles until he fell down bleeding. A rumor had been going around that the Koreans had started the fires, poisoned wells, and done other evil things. Because of the rumors, quite a few Koreans were killed. Many had to be taken into "protective custody."

At one stop the trains changed engines, so I tried to find a better seat on the new engine. First I helped a woman with a small child get into the train through a window, and then I left the crowded platform. As soon as the new engine came down the track I got a fine seat on the cowcatcher out in front, but the engineer came along and said, "You may be able to ride the cowcatcher in America, but not in Japan!" I had to squeeze back into the coal car instead.

Another station was crowded with people who had been taken off the roofs of previous trains because of the tunnels which were ahead on the tracks. After a miserable night, we reached Karuizawa about daybreak. At the Karuizawa station I found a group of young men with poles and hooks, trying to catch Koreans! I told them to go home, that all the talk about Koreans was only rumor.

At Karuizawa folks were busy taking cooked rice balls and sandwiches to the station to give to the refugees on the packed trains. A few days later I took my bicycle and started for our home in Mito. I knew I would never be able to get my bicycle aboard the trains going through Karuizawa, so I rode to a small station on a side line which went part way toward Mito. Here I climbed onto the roof of a boxcar with my bike. It was a comfortable, but smoky ride. Later on I was able to get inside a boxcar.

At one station where I knew the stationmaster, I got off the train to run back and tell him his relatives in Tokyo were all right. Some firemen with long poles began running after me shouting, *"Senjin!"* meaning "Korean!" Because of my long legs I was able to reach the stationmaster ahead of them. He immediately stood me against the train, placed himself in front of me with his arms outstretched to protect me, and shouted that I was an American, his friend. Then he asked two of the men who had been chasing me to be my bodyguards the rest of the way to Mito!

There was no serious damage in Mito, so after reporting to the folks there about the situation in Tokyo, I again started for Tokyo on my bicycle with a load of rice in a sidecar for the refugees. This time I rode through a different section of Tokyo on my way to the Friends' compound. I passed a park into which 35,000 people had fled with their belongings when the earthquake struck. But the fires that resulted from the quake completely surrounded the park. They and all their goods perished. In the main business section of the city a nine-story concrete building under construction had buckled, killing 200 workmen.

I spent several days in Tokyo helping wherever I could. Food and building supplies began to arrive from the Philippines, so we were able to help build a barrack village for refugees in a nearby park. When there was nothing left for me to do to help, I returned to Karuizawa for Madeline and baby Virginia, and we returned home to Mito.

Friends in Karuizawa told us that their mission's girls' school in Yokohama had been completely destroyed by the earthquake, and the principal of the school had died in the fire. We were asked if we would take the servants of the teachers' residence and give them temporary lodging until there was another place for them to go.

We agreed to help them. The parents came to work for us, bringing their three children, a grandmother, and an aunt. We had a very happy year with this family living with us and have continued our friendship through the years.

Chapter 8

Japan Years

In the summer of 1924, my mother came to Japan to be with us when our second child was born. That event took place at Karuizawa in the late afternoon of June 24. I walked down the hill with Madeline to the nursing home just in time. An American nurse got her ready while I ran after the doctor and nurse that we had engaged. I found the doctor having tea in one of the cottages and the nurse in the public bath! I got back ahead of them and was holding Madeline's hands, trying to help, when the doctor rushed in just in time to welcome our son, Samuel. Donald was also born at Karuizawa, three years later on September 4, 1927.

Many years before we came to Mito, the Friends' mission had bought a piece of land outside town, intending to build a boys' school there. The school never materialized, so the land was traded for an acre just across the fields from the new Mito Junior College. Madeline and I were still interested in getting into rural work. We felt that this place might be just the place for us. The mission agreed.

We sent word to the board that we would like to take a short trip to America at our own expense in time for the golden wedding anniversary of Madeline's parents. I also wished to go to Philadelphia to raise funds for a new home and a small student's dormitory in our new location. We sold Madeline's piano for enough money to buy our round-trip ticket to California and to get me to Philadelphia.

We were in Pasadena by New Year's Day, 1926. After a couple of weeks I went on to Philadelphia alone. I found that the mission board was financially in the red and that there was much fear that I might make matters worse if I were given permission to raise the $4,500 Madeline and I needed in Japan. Things looked hopeless until a good friend of mine said, "Turn Herbert loose with his enthusiasm, and he'll not only raise this money but get us out of the red as well!"

That turned the tables. I was given permission to try for one week, but not to actually take in any money—only pledges. At the end of the week I was to report back to the finance committee about my success.

The next morning I went to the home of my friend George Williams, where I found that a famous Quaker evangelist, Charles Stalker, was visiting. I told these men why I was in Philadelphia. The three of us got on our knees and spent the morning in prayer.

On the train to Atlantic City that afternoon, I felt in my heart that I would be able to raise $1,000 from the wealthy Quaker hotel men. But when I arrived I discovered that they were all very hard pressed financially, and I received only $250 in pledges that evening. One of the men whom I had hoped could help, Walter Buzby, invited me to spend the night at his hotel, the *Dennis*. We had breakfast together, and then he suggested that I go up to his wife's room and tell her everything I had just told him. He advised me that she was not well, however, so I must not stay long.

Mrs. Emily Buzby told me the same thing, that money was very tight and she was sorry she could not give to the mission board the way she used to. In view of her situation, I told her not to worry about my need, but to give all she could to the board.

I must admit I was becoming discouraged. I was supposed to take the train back to Philadelphia right after lunch. At lunch, a waiter came and told me that the hotel manager wished to see me before I left. When I went into his office, he handed me an important-looking paper and said that Mrs. Buzby had told him to give it to me. It turned out to be a government bond worth $1,030! I said I wasn't supposed to take any money, only pledges, and could I talk to Mrs. Buzby. "No," he said. "She's resting now. And anyhow, she won't change her mind!"

Pledges for the mission began coming in from various Friends' communities. One evening the Moorestown Friends called a special meeting. It was a stormy night and another meeting was being held in town to which many Friends went, so there was not a large crowd. I talked about our work in Japan, about our dreams, but said nothing about money. After my talk someone else got up, told about our need of a new home, and then passed the hat around—not a very Quakerly thing to do!

I had told a very close friend, Bess Roberts, that the Lord had promised me a $1,000 for that evening. She replied that it was absolutely impossible since none of the really wealthy Friends were there. Later that night she called me to find out how much money had come in. I replied, "According to your faith, be it unto you." When I added the cash and checks that had been slipped into my pockets to what the treasurer reported, it just made a $1,000!

Before going to the meeting of the finance committee back in Philadelphia the next day, I had lunch with Mrs. Robert B. Haines, Jr. in Germantown and told her the purpose of my trip. As I was leaving she said, "Herbert, $4,500 is not enough. When all the money promised is in, let me know and I'll make up the total to $5,000."

At the finance committee meeting, the treasurer informed us that $4,500 had been paid or pledged for our new home in Japan, and in addition, the mission board accounts were in the black for the first time in months.

Thus, it was a very thankful, happy young man who returned to Pasadena to join in the golden wedding celebrations for Father and Mother Waterhouse. The Lake Avenue Congregational Church had a special meeting in their honor. They also gave Madeline and me a wonderful "shower" to help furnish our new home.

Upon our arrival back in Mito we began at once to build and to prepare the grounds. We had excellent frontage on a provincial road out of Mito. Later the area was taken into the city and called *Higashi Hara machi* (East Field Street). Our two-story house was built on a hill at the rear of the property overlooking a valley through which the railway from Tokyo ran. Beyond were beautiful woods. At the front of the property, we built a small gatehouse and behind that, a two-story dormitory that would hold five or six students. In September of 1926 we moved into our new home. This began a new era of our lives in Japan.

About 6 a.m. a few days after we moved, I went out into the garden with my Bible and sat in meditation. These words came to me in the quiet, "Nothing between but Jesus. Nothing between you and your wife and the children but the Spirit of Jesus. Nothing between you and your fellow workers but Christ. Nothing between you and God but the broken body of Christ." I opened my Bible, and my eyes fell upon these words:

> *Having therefore, brethren, boldness to enter into the holiest by the blood of Jesus, by a new and living way, which he hath consecrated for us,*

through the veil, that is to say, his flesh. (Hebrews
10:19, 20)

These words moved me deeply. It is by the broken body of
Christ that we come into the presence of our Heavenly
Father. "Nothing between but Jesus."

I'll have to admit that during the next years I did not
always fully reach this ideal. Too often things did come between. But this deep spiritual experience made a difference
in my life. The next time I met one of the men who had created a lot of hard feelings in the Mito meeting, I took hold of
his hand, looked him straight in the eye and said nothing.
He returned my look and squeezed my hand hard. The love
of Jesus passed between us, and from that day our relation-
ship was different.

During the next thirteen years in Japan, there were many
crises and serious problems, but it was my prayer that each
one might be met in the Spirit of Christ. They were happy
years in our family and very important ones for our growing
children.

Our home was built on a hill facing the south. Nearly all
the rooms received an abundance of God's sunshine
through the cold winter days, and what a lovely view we
had! The land surrounding ours was mostly pear orchards
and wheatland, with farmhouses scattered about where
there were many children.

At the side of the road, to the right of our gate, was a tiny
house where weary travelers could rest or get out of the rain.
Inside our gate there was room for vegetable and flower
gardens, chicken and goat houses, and, in addition to the
gatehouse, the kindergarten and Sunday school building,
the tramps' lodge, the dormitory and coworkers' house. We
had lots of strawberries, raspberries, asparagus, and
rhubarb.

The children were always interested in animals, especially Snowhopper, our first little goat. One time they counted 57 pets on our property, including the snake in the garden!

I believe our children had a happy home life. When they were old enough, they all had bicycles and we often took rides together. They attended our Sunday school and went to the Friends' meeting in Mito. Samuel even started his own Sunday school at our nearest train station, Akatsuka.

Madeline never turned the children over to anyone else for their schooling. She taught them all herself, using the accredited Calvert correspondence school program.

One time when I spanked Donald, he climbed up on my lap crying and said, "Daddy, let's work by the law of love and kisses!" There was very little spanking.

We had many overnight guests in our home, and we had a rule that the children could have half an hour alone with them if at all possible. Gilbert and Minnie Bowles were frequent guests and Gilbert, whom the children called "uncle," always took them into my study, sat on the couch with one child on each side and one in front, and they would read the big unabridged dictionary!

When Rufus Jones of Haverford College and his wife Elizabeth came to Japan, they spent a weekend with us. At our family worship Rufus prayed that each of our children might find the "trail of life." He had just written a little book called *Finding the Trail of Life*.

The famous Japanese social worker, Toyohiko Kagawa and his wife also visited us, as well as the blind evangelist Takeo Iwahashi.

We made every attempt to be friends with all the missionaries in our area. There were several missionary families of the Church of Christ in rural districts near ours, and they often came to our house for Thanksgiving dinner. The Presbyterian and Baptist pastors met with us for monthly pastors' meetings, and we worked together in special New

Year prayer meetings and also in street meetings, especially in the spring when there were excursion groups from Tokyo to see the plum blossoms. We were also friendly with the Catholic, Episcopalian, and Holiness pastors.

Our main concern, of course, was evangelism. Our province was very traditional and conservative, and it was difficult to lead folks to Christ. We put much of our strength into the Mito Friends' meeting, attending their regular services as a family, but we also had our own Sunday school. Some of the students who lived in our little dormitory had become Christians and they helped as Sunday school teachers. We also had children's meetings in three villages. At this time I was still doing some teaching and had my weekly Bible class as well.

We had always felt that rural work involved special considerations different from missionary work in schools or in the cities. Mr. Fujisaki, a rural worker for the well-known social worker Kagawa, also recognized this fact. He began a movement called *Shinseikai,* "New Life Societies." This movement was directed specifically toward rural people and spread all over Japan.

My predecessor at Mito, Gurney Binford, was keenly interested in the *Shinseikai* project. One of the early converts from his Bible class later resigned from a respected position as principal of a primary school in order to give full time to the project in our province.

Each winter four or five small conferences were held for the farmers involved in the local program. We had one in our kindergarten building to which eight or nine young men came. The pastor of the Mito meeting, Senjiro Kameyama, conducted the daily Bible study. Mr. Fujisaki, the founder, would usually come for at least part of the time and, on one occasion, even Kagawa himself spent a day with us.

We were also interested in providing practical help to the young farmers in our area. One thing we did was start a savings account for them. Each month they would deposit a small amount in the post office. They could borrow from this to buy day-old chicks, or a goat, for example. One group bought a rice-hulling machine and went about their village hulling rice for their neighbors. We also set up a cooperative store in Mito to which the young men delivered eggs, rice, and vegetables.

And then we became involved in the goat business. I've already mentioned one of our pets, Snowhopper. The children loved her on sight and improved in health just by playing with her. Unfortunately, her pen was blown over the hedge in a severe storm just about the time she was ready to kid, and poor Snowhopper died.

Not long afterward, Mr. Bixler, a rural missionary and a great goat enthusiast, arrived at our place with a goat and two kids in the rumble seat of his car! He gave us instructions about how to feed them, and we tasted our first goat's milk. We became so enthusiastic about goat's milk that we decided to go into the business so we could help others who needed milk. Susumu Yamaguchi, one of the young farmers of the *Shinseikai*, came to live with us to run our goat dairy.

The goat center of Japan at that time was near Karuizawa, our summer home in the mountains, so each summer on our way there we would buy about twenty goats and take them with us. We would milk them for the two months while there, selling the milk to the other missionaries for their children. By the end of the summer we always had made enough money to pay for the goats. Then we took them back with us to Mito, where Susumu took charge. Those goats which did not give much milk were sold at low prices to our *Shinseikai* farmers. The rest we kept for our dairy.

We were also involved in a number of projects connected with the mission work, such as the Temperance Society in Mito. Historically Quakers have been involved in temperance movements, and our Mito meeting was no exception. The Presbyterians and the Baptists also participated.

The Friends' mission in Mito owned two pieces of land which were sold for the temperance project. With the money received, a splendid lot on the main street of town was purchased. The Temperance Society built a fine three-story building which contained a cooperative store, a matrimonial bureau, a place where one could get free legal advice, a Christian sewing school, and in the rear, a day nursery for the children of shopkeepers.

Another project we had was putting religious advertisements into our local newspaper. For some years we did this, following up all the letters that came in response. One time we received seventy letters from one ad. In the follow-up we discovered that practically all who wrote to us had tuberculosis. In fact, the whole situation regarding tuberculosis in our area was of great concern to us.

Before World War II, there was a great deal of tuberculosis throughout Japan. We discovered, however, that the doctors did not call the disease tuberculosis when they discovered a case because it would bring disgrace to the family.

One of the men from the Mito meeting wanted to find a piece of property on which to build a sanatorium. We found an ideal spot on a hill above Onuki, but local feeling against a TB sanatorium was so strong that the farmer who owned the land refused to sell it for that purpose. The same thing happened at Muramatsu. So our plans fell through. But after the war both these places had hospitals.

Leprosy was another problem. One Easter Sunday on my way to the park in Mito to talk to the crowds who came from Tokyo to see the plum blossoms, I stopped in one of the caves by the railroad track to visit a young man who lived there. I had to crawl on my hands and knees until the cave became higher. When my eyes became accustomed to the dark and smoke, I could see a one-legged man cooking rice and a young man sitting nearby. This young man had leprosy.

He was an earnest Christian, and I often gave him tracts and Testaments to distribute to people. His face was badly marked and both hands and feet were mere stumps. He had a small homemade cart with tiny wooden wheels in which he sat with his baggage, propelled by pushing his bandaged hands on the ground.

He asked me once if he would have this leprosy-maimed body when the resurrection came for him. I assured him that whatever future life had in store for him, it surely would not be a body like he had now!

On this particular Sunday he told me that he would like to get to Kumamoto where there was a Christian leprosarium run by an English missionary. I told him I would go to the police to try to find a way for him to get there.

The next day I did some investigating and found, to my surprise, that there was no record of leprosy cases in our province! Apparently the police were required to send any patients they found to a leprosarium near Tokyo. Since that was too much trouble, they deliberately avoided seeing beggars with the disease, although at that time we would often see lepers begging at the temple gates.

I went back to the cave to tell my friend that I wanted to make him a cart with bicycle wheels that would run more easily, and that I would help him on his way to Kumamoto. But when I got to the cave I found that the young man, afraid that the police would catch him and send him to Tokyo, had left at once on his own.

A week later I received a postcard from a town about thirty miles away on which was written a Japanese poem which went something like this:

It's evening.
I see
over the rice fields
lights in homes.
And here I am so lonely.

The following October, nearly six months after he had started from Mito, I received a letter from the leprosarium telling me that my friend had finally reached Kumamoto and was happy to be with Christians.

During the Depression in the early thirties, many tramps came to our door. With a gift of $50 that had been sent us by the Sunday school of Lake Avenue Congregational Church, we built a six-mat (about nine by twelve feet) lodge where we could provide lodging for these people for the night. In the morning, after spending the night with us, each guest would receive three balls of rice with a dried plum in the center. Then I would send them on their way with a word of advice and the "Good News."

One Sunday morning two tramps came while we were having Sunday school. I had a short talk with them and they left with rice balls. That afternoon one of them returned to talk with me. He said that he had lied to me in the morning. When he heard the children singing "Jesus Loves Me" as he left, something happened inside him. His name was Shimamura. He had been a tramp for seventeen years.

I told Shimamura he could spend the night with us and the next morning we would go into business together. In the morning I gave him a yen and introductions to the churches in Mito. With the yen he bought a bottle of creosote, a bucket, and a brush, and then went about cleaning toilets. That evening he returned and paid back the yen!

About this time our gardener became sick and died of cancer, so we asked Shimamura to be our gardener and tramp teacher. He never drank again after hearing the children's hymn, but it took him two years to quit smoking.

Every January first we had a special New Year's breakfast for our workers and boys. After eating, everyone would make New Year's resolutions. Each year Shimamura told us he would stop smoking, but he soon would begin again secretly. Finally, after one of these breakfasts, Shimamura said he wanted to talk to me privately. We went into my study. He told me that just before Christmas he was going out to the woods to get a Christmas tree. He had left three cigarettes on his *kotatsu* (charcoal heater). When he came back, three little girls from his Sunday school class were sitting warming their feet in his *kotatsu,* each with a lit cigarette! That settled it. He was through forever. And he kept that resolve.

Years later when we left Japan in 1940, Mr. Hirakawa, principal of the Friends' Girls' School in Tokyo, remarked to us as he saw us off at the dock, that our life in Japan had been worthwhile just to have won Shimamura to Christ.

One night an old man slept in our lodge. As I saw him leave the next day, all bent over and walking with his cane, I called him back and told him to stay another night with us. He was very hard of hearing and could hardly see. We found that he had been married to a very difficult young woman, and being unable to get along with her had run away from home. He finally became a *goto* (knife-carrying burglar), and had served a total of thirty years in the penitentiary. Now he had nowhere to go. We could not send him away, so we kept him busy helping with the gardening and pumping water. Everyone soon called him "Grandpa" Minagawa, and he became the first member of our old folks' home.

We had felt for some time that there was a need for some place for old folks like Grandpa Minagawa. We had bought a piece of land a mile out in the country that had two small houses on it. We gave one of the houses to the family that used to live in our gatehouse, and decided to use the other for a home for old folks.

We then searched the province for homeless old people, but could find only five or six who would come to live in our old folks' home, in spite of the fact that there were no such institutions anywhere in Ibaraki Ken. Tradition had it that every family was to take care of its own grandparents. Only those who had no family at all would come in.

One night the small house on our property burned down. Grandpa Minagawa had a way of getting angry at least once a month, and we think he set fire to the place while temporarily mad. It was obvious that if we were to have an old people's home, we needed not only a roof over their heads, but also some supervision.

In 1935 a "Fact Finding Commission" that was sent around the world by John D. Rockefeller, Jr. came to Japan. They visited us and became interested in our efforts to start a home for old people who had nowhere to go. Because of their visit, we were given a grant to continue what we had begun. That same year we also received a grant from the Mitsubishi Company. We decided to use the money to build a home for about twenty people. This time it would be on the grounds of our own home. Shimamura became the superintendent of the home, and we were able to fill it with old people.

Chapter 9

War Clouds

After our 1935 furlough, things began to change for us. War clouds were gathering over the whole world. As the Japanese invasion of China progressed, I was looked upon with suspicion as a possible American spy. About once a month two plainclothesmen came from the police station to find out what I thought of the Manchurian Incident and the invasion of China. The Mito police station had quite a book on Nicholson's "thoughts" before they were through!

Whenever I visited out in the country a plainclothesman would always secretly follow me about. After I left he would visit every home I had visited to find out everything I had said. This became very embarrassing and difficult for my friends, so I was forced to stop calling on them.

Censorship became so strict throughout Japan that the people really had no knowledge at all of what was going on in China. Japanese agents in America read all the magazines as they came off the presses, and if any particular issue had too much in it about China, that number was confiscated when it reached Japan. I received *The Christian Century* each week, sent to me by a friend who read it first and then mailed it to me. It was one publication that was often destroyed because it had much in it that came from missionaries who were in China. My copy generally escaped confiscation because it always arrived a few days later than the regular subscriptions. Sometimes I would take these papers to the pastors' meetings, but they could hardly believe what they read.

Because of the air of suspicion that hung about me, even the pastors had to ask me not to attend their meetings any more. When I had been there, the police always came afterward and asked what I had talked about.

Finally one morning early in 1939, a member of the Friends' mission board came from Tokyo to see us. He took me aside into the garden and gently broke the news that the board, which was financially hard pressed because of the economic depression at home, would have to drop us. He was very relieved when I told him that Madeline and I had already decided to resign. Since it was becoming impossible for us to work out in the countryside without creating suspicion, we felt it was time to consider returning home to America. Moreover, our children, Virginia and Samuel, whom we had left in school in America after our last furlough, needed us.

It was agreed that by summer we would be ready to leave Japan. The board was to pay our way back to the States and we would receive our salary until the end of the year.

But when spring came that year, the Canadian Academy in Kobe asked us to take charge of the boys' dormitory and teach in the School. After 25 years away from the classroom, I did not feel qualified to teach, but Madeline went to Kobe anyway to look over the situation. When she returned she said she felt it would be right to take the job, so we accepted.

After completing our year with the school, we were asked to remain another year, but this time Madeline and I felt we should return to America. We sold our piano, typewriter, and other furniture and sailed for home on the new *Nitta Maru*, third class.

Gradually we settled into our new life in Pasadena, California. The opportunity to serve the West Los Angeles Japanese Methodist Church opened. Through these happy days, though we knew of the possibility of war with Japan, we did not at all anticipate how quickly the war clouds that hung over us in Japan would fall on us again in America.

Then came that fateful day, December 7, 1941, when the Japanese war planes flew in over the great naval base on Oahu. Below them, totally unprepared for the attack, lay the Pacific fleet of the United States Navy. Just minutes before, the Japanese had hit the Hawaiian air fields in order to eliminate any possible interference from the air. Now the ninety-some ships in Pearl Harbor lay unprotected.

The Japanese force was in two groups—an advance force of over 30 submarines and some 200 planes. An additional striking force of over 300 planes from six aircraft followed.

Most of the damage, both to American aircraft and ships, occurred during the first few minutes of the attack, which began at 7:55 a.m. Hawaii time. At 8:10 the *Arizona* blew up with more than a thousand men on board. Lined up with it in "battleship row" were the *California, Oklahoma,* and *West Virginia* which also received direct hits almost immediately. The attack ended shortly before 10 a.m.

There was confusion, smoke, and flames everywhere. The harbor was full of sunk and heavily damaged ships. When the attack ended, men worked feverishly to save what they could of planes, ships, and men and to prepare for the next attack.

Honolulu, and the rest of the country as it heard the news, waited all that day and into the night for the return of the enemy planes. But they did not come. The Japanese military leadership, anxious not to overstep its luck, called its planes home in spite of the eagerness of many of the men to continue the attack.

The Japanese losses and casualties were slight, but the cost to the United States was the lives of hundreds of officers and men, several great battleships, and many smaller vessels. Hundreds of aircraft were damaged or destroyed. It was a crushing blow!

The news of Pearl Harbor was as much a shock to the Japanese American communities of Hawaii and of the West Coast as to the rest of the country. Although the moods of the Japanese had fluctuated back and forth with the state of relations between America and Japan, *nobody* was prepared for the attack. This cannot be emphasized enough.

The general reaction among Americans after the initial shock wore off was outrage at the Japanese ambassadors, Kichisaburo Nomura and Saburo Kurusu. They were seen as deliberately misleading the American people into thinking that Japan would not attack us. History has since shown that this was not the case. Relations between Japan and the United States had been steadily deteriorating. Nomura and Kurusu were continually advising President Franklin Roosevelt that certain actions, such as the enactment of economic sanctions against Japan, were certain to bring war. Their warnings were ignored, but the American people knew nothing of this.

The outrage over the surprise attack directed at the Japanese ambassadors in Washington was extended to the Japanese at home. "You can't trust a Jap," and "Once a Jap always a Jap," seemed to be confirmed by the supposed behavior of those two notorious "Japs" in Washington.

The great irony is that Ambassador Nomura had worked ceaselessly to maintain a state of peace between the United States and Japan. A known admirer of the United States and Britain, he was trapped between an extremist military group in Japan which had come into power, and an administration in Washington which would not heed his advice.

Nomura was not the only one who was warning the President. The United States ambassador to Japan, Joseph C. Grew, had long been aware of the direction of the relations between the two countries. He saw the coming of war as tragic but inevitable. Yet, he hoped that the status quo in the Pacific might be maintained, at least until the war in Europe had been won or lost.

As early as April of 1941, Ambassador Nomura had told President Roosevelt that Prime Minister Konoye felt so strongly about maintaining peaceful relations between the United States and Japan that he would be willing to meet with the President someplace geographically midway between the two countries. This request for a meeting was repeated again and again. Ambassador Grew personally appealed for "very prayerful consideration" of it.

But President Roosevelt stalled. Finally he said that a meeting might be arranged for sometime in October, 1941. Nomura stressed the urgency of an earlier date. On August 27, Prime Minister Konoye sent a personal appeal to the President for a meeting "as soon as possible."

But then Secretary of State Cordell Hull raised the objection that before there could be a meeting between the two leaders, some preliminary agreements would have to be worked out in order to insure a successful outcome. Roosevelt further insisted that Japan halt her expansionist activities in French Indo-China before he could meet with Konoye.

Matters drifted along until mid-October, when the final date proposed by the Japanese, had passed. The hopes of the Japanese moderates had been pinned on that meeting. It would have given them an edge against the increasing pressures of the military extremists who were gaining political strength in Japan. When the meeting failed to take place, they could no longer hold back the tide. On October 16, the Konoye cabinet resigned and General Tojo and the militarists took over the government.

All this time Washington had led the public and press to believe that as long as the negotiations continued there was still substantial hope of preserving peace. The public did not know that the negotiations had already come to an abrupt end in October. For years afterward the story was carefully cultivated that the Japanese attack was a treacherous surprise and therefore a great shock to the leaders of our government.

For the Japanese American community, the Pearl Harbor disaster could not have come at a worse time. Decades of racist and anti-Oriental propaganda, plus an irrational fear of Oriental conquest which the Hearst newspapers and others like them had been creating in the public mind for some 40 years, provided a fertile environment for the events of the next months and years. The shock of the attack on Pearl Harbor merely served to bring to a head the long-standing tension.

The first few weeks that followed Pearl Harbor, after the initial wave of "precautionary" arrests, were relatively calm despite genuine fear of an attack from outside. Then, after the turn of the year 1942, when Japan's alarming successes in the Pacific continued, pressure began to build on the West Coast for the removal of all Japanese.

Particularly vocal on the issue of evacuation were groups that had a commercial advantage to gain by the elimination of Japanese competition. These included the California American Legion, the Grower-shipper Vegetable Association, the California Farm Bureau Federation, the Western Growers Protective Association, gardener's organizations, and similar groups characterized by a long history of hostility against the Japanese.

The press was another source of agitation for evacuation.

Charges of sabotage and espionage were frequently in the headlines. Japanese nationalistic organizations were said to be part of an effective "fifth column" at work, and in many such ways the press day after day stirred up the fires of fear, racism, and hatred.

Unfortunately for the Japanese Americans, the attack on Pearl Harbor was viewed by the public and press as a sneak attack. After the war it was explained that an error in procedure had delayed the official notice from Japan terminating negotiations from reaching the State Department in Washington in time. Until then, the press and general public concluded that sabotage, based on the cooperation of Japanese in Hawaii and on the mainland, had made the surprise attack possible.

This was a great injustice. None of the charges of sabotage or collaboration had any basis in fact. No resident Japanese living either in Hawaii or on the mainland was ever convicted of being an agent of Japan, or of having been involved in either sabotage or espionage.

Chapter 10

Evacuation

On February 19, 1942, President Franklin Delano Roosevelt signed Executive Order 9066 which authorized the removal of "any and all persons" from strategic areas. John L. DeWitt, Commanding General of the Western Defense Command, issued Proclamation 1 on March 2 which ordered all persons of "Japanese ancestry" from the western half of the three Pacific states and the southern third of Arizona.

By contrast, the Japanese were not ordered out of Hawaii *en masse*. Since they were the single largest national group on the islands, their removal would have meant a massive reduction of the labor force at a time when every able-bodied hand was needed, so a sense of self-preservation prevailed. Instead, the islands were put under martial law.

My own involvement in the evacuation was so hectic that I cannot possibly tell the story chronologically. I shall just tell a few of my experiences with this tragic bit of history.

In late January the Army declared some ninety areas, most near military bases, harbors, and air fields, as "strategic," and therefore out-of-bounds to all citizens of the Axis powers. All German, Italian, and Japanese aliens were asked to move out of these areas. A good number of Japanese attempted to comply by moving from the coast inland. Some even moved beyond the border of California. The Friend's Service Committee, for which I worked for a time, helped quite a few families make this move.

One group of farmers who had originally lived along the shore north of San Pedro moved to virgin land in the foothills of the Sierra Nevada mountains near Porterville, California. They spent a lot of money to build makeshift housing, dig wells, and clear the land. When all this was finished, they planted acres and acres of tomatoes. When the order for the military removal of all Japanese came, these farmers were forced to go to relocation centers before they had picked a single tomato. What a waste of food supplies in wartime!

Toward the end of February, I was sitting one day in a meeting of the Friends' Service Committee, when suddenly I had a very strong feeling that I should go to Terminal Island at once. When I arrived I discovered that the Japanese residents of Terminal Island, about five hundred fishermen and a few others, were about to be told that they had exactly forty-eight hours in which to get out! The Japanese community on the island was considered too close to a naval base for national security.

We got on the telephone at once to inform the Southern California Japanese Church Federation and others. We asked them to send delegates at once to the Terminal Island church for a meeting.

That afternoon quite a group gathered at the church. We made plans to help the Japanese with transportation, places to stay, and the handling of their belongings, whether to be stored or sold. Many of the Issei fathers of the families on Terminal Island had earlier been arrested by the FBI, so the wives had to manage the selling of their household furniture and find places to stay all on their own. Everyone who had a place to go had already left the island. They were fortunate. Those who were left were in difficult straits.

The next morning Terminal Island was crowded with many friends who came to help, and also profiteers who came to get something for nothing. Trouble seems to bring out the best and worst in people.

As warclouds gathered, a great many Buddhists had begun to attend services at the Japanese Baptist Church, thinking that as Christians they would be better treated in a national emergency. This turned out to be true. The Japanese Christians had more Caucasian friends, and most of the church people were interested in helping only people of their own denominations. I remember very clearly the Baptist superintendent saying to me, "We'll take care of the Baptists, and the Quakers can look after the Buddhists."

Only a small minority of Caucasian Christians tried to live the Sermon on the Mount that day by being impartial in their efforts to help all who were in need. The Moody Mattress Company sent its trucks to help in the moving, and Quaker farmers and pastors in workclothes also brought trucks. My old friends, Elizabeth and Gurney Binford, spent two days helping the Ishii family liquidate their drugstore stock. And the assistant pastor from Hollywood Congregational Church, though crippled, came to help pack the hymn books and Bibles for the local church.

I went into a beer hall run by a woman whose husband had been put into detention and found a man from the Board of Equalization going through her account books while she was busy trying to pack. Her records were in very poor shape. He attached her property so she could not sell anything. Everything was lost. It was very sad.

Within weeks after the general evacuation order was issued on March 2, the Japanese began to be moved under military guard to assembly centers, temporary quarters at race tracks or fair grounds, since the relocation centers (with the exception of Manzanar) were not yet built. My wife and I often visited the Santa Anita Assembly Center where our friends were being housed in horse stables. Several thousand people were put in these stables, though there had been only a four-day interval between the hurried evacuation of the horses and the arrival of the people. There was still the distinct odor of the previous tenants, in spite of the fact that the stalls had been hosed down and sprayed with disinfectant before being hastily whitewashed. During the summer months the stench was terrible. Another inconvenience of stable living was that privacy was difficult to maintain. The "walls" between the "rooms" were, of course, only horse high.

Very often people lived in the assembly centers a couple of months before being sent on to the more permanent relocation camps. I remember very clearly the day we took a birthday cake to Santa Anita for old Mr. Hiraiwa. When we arrived at the gate of the Center with the birthday cake in a bakery box, the guard who inspected all packages tore open the box and stuck a rusty knife into the cake several times. When I objected he replied, "There might be a bomb in the cake!"

Many times during the next three months we were at stations or assembly points to see folks off on their long bus trips. The Quakers and other church groups were always on hand to help with baggage and to serve coffee and doughnuts. The Japanese were allowed to take only what they could carry in their hands, and since most had already sold or given away their cars, they had no way to get to the send-off point with their baggage. Fortunately, many Caucasian friends volunteered their help.

Not everyone was so generous, however. I remember one time seeing a truck with a hospital's name painted on the side standing at a station. I asked the driver if he wouldn't come and help, since there was lots of baggage yet to be brought. But he coolly replied, "We've brought all our people."

We were especially active helping our own church people from West Los Angeles. The chapel there was converted into a warehouse with furniture piled almost to the ceiling. The last service we held was a sad one. No one knew just what was ahead. Madeline and I accompanied our people to the bus to see them off to the Manzanar Relocation Center, not knowing when we would see them again. We expected that this would end our income from these dear folks, but they continued to send us $30 for several months.

In May we saw the last group off at a bus station. They were headed for Arizona. I noticed on this occasion some Caucasian men who were standing by the bus and their wives and children who were on board, obviously being sent away. Upon investigating the situation, I found out the story.

Many years earlier, a Russian lady had married a Japanese man and they had several children. The husband died when the children were infants. The mother married again and had more children. The first set of children had been so young when their father died that they were raised as children of their mother's second husband. They didn't know their real father was Japanese until one of the girls tried to get a war job and the authorities probed into her background. Now she and her children were being taken away from her husband, along with her sister and her sister's children, to be sent into the desert with the rest of the Japanese!

After the bus left I took the two husbands of these women to see Colonel Severence in Pasadena. I had had many dealings with him, and although he was a rather hard-fisted military man, I knew he had a heart. When we were allowed to see him and explained the situation he exploded, "Well, this is out-Hitlering Hitler!"

He flew to Washington to try to straighten out the mess. Nevertheless, it was six weeks before the women and their children were brought back home.

By August over 110,000 persons had been interned by the government without charge or trial. The only criterion of their removal was the fact that they had been born of Japanese parents. Most of these people remained excluded from their homes, property, and communities for nearly three years. Some were deported, never to return. Seventy thousand of them, nearly two-thirds the total, were American citizens, born on United States soil. The other forty thousand, with few exceptions, were Japanese who had lived in the United States for many years, some as long as forty years, but were ineligible for citizenship under the immigration practices of our country. It was a terrible injustice and a violation of the constitutional right of all people to due process of law.

Before long we began to receive letters from our friends at Manzanar wanting us to come see them. I wrote that we would come as soon as we could get permission. I was anxious to see the place myself, especially to see under what conditions our people were living.

It was July before we were able to get the necessary permission to visit Manzanar. We rented a stake truck and loaded it with pianos, hymn books, benches, and pulpits for the churches, and other things the Japanese had written they needed. We also went to the Los Angeles Public Library and got a great many discarded books. Then, Madeline and I started out over the Angeles Crest Highway on the 200-mile trek to Manzanar.

Just after we went through Lancaster in the desert, the two rear tires blew out. I had quite a time getting them off and hitchhiking with them back to Lancaster to have them fixed. Madeline stayed with the truck in the burning desert heat without even water to drink, while back in Lancaster I had lunch in the air-conditioned home of our friends, Mr. and Mrs. Floyd Lorbeer. Poor Madeline! She managed to get a book out from between the slats in the back of the truck so at least she had something to read.

When I returned to the truck with lunch for Madeline, Mr. Lorbeer went with us. We got on our way again, but a few miles from Lone Pine the tires blew out again. Fortunately, this time we were right by a filling station. Since it was dark when we reached Lone Pine, we decided to stop at a motel and get a good night's rest before going on. The next morning we were soon involved in the formalities of going through the gate of the camp.

Our first impression of Manzanar was memorable. The place was absolutely desolate. Although it was only a little more than 200 miles from Los Angeles, it gave the appearance of being in the middle of nowhere, completely remote and uninhabited except for the artificial city of barracks that had been thrown up to house the evacuees. At the gate into the camp were administration buildings and some neat little cottages for the staff. To the right of the entrance and beyond stretched block after block of black tar paper-covered barracks. The dust, blown by the wind into every crack and crevice, inside and out of the buildings, waged a continual battle against the determined housewives.

Manzanar was one of ten so-called "relocation" camps, all in remote hot desert or wasteland areas: Manzanar and Tule Lake in California; Poston and Gila River, both on Indian reservations in Arizona; Topaz in central Utah; Amache in Colorado; Heart Mountain in Wyoming; Minidoka in Idaho; and Rohwer and Jerome in Arkansas. All the camps were bound by barbed wire and guarded by sentries with machine guns in high towers.

Manzanar was built to hold 10,000 people, a small city, one mile square. There were about 40 blocks of barracks, each containing twelve 20 x 100 foot barracks. In each block the buildings were lined up in two rows with lavatories, showers, and laundry rooms situated in the center. The barracks for living quarters were divided into five, 20 x 20 foot rooms. Five people were assigned to each room. Families of five were fortunate, because then they would not have to share their room with others, or be divided up. With no partitions and only one small light bulb in the center of the ceiling, these rooms were hardly adequate for family living! There was practically no furniture. Each person was given a ticking sack in which they stuffed straw for a mattress. There were supposed to be cots as well, but often they were missing, or came later.

Eventually, many of the internees were given the option of moving east. The Nisei college students were the earliest afforded this opportunity. This made a little more room for everyone else so that conditions were not as crowded as they might have been.

When we arrived at the gate, the man in charge of recreation, Axel Nielson, met us and directed us to the section where the West Los Angeles folks were. We received a wonderful welcome from our friends. Everyone excitedly helped us unload the pianos, benches, and hymn books at the recreation barracks which were also to be used for churches, libraries, and schools. We had one piano for the West Los Angeles church and another piano and an organ for the two other churches.

When the truck was unloaded, Nielson took us to the administration building to introduce us to Manzanar's director, Mr. Roy Nash. In doing so, Nielson said to Nash, "These people belong in this camp to help us!" Without hesitation, Mr. Nash offered us any job we would like. It was a generous gesture, but I had to tell him that since I was personally very opposed to the evacuation, I could not in any way be a partner in the affair. I wished to be free so that I could fight the whole evacuation idea. We had other interests outside of Manzanar as well, such as helping the sick, and helping friends in other camps. Besides, I could not conscientiously accept a large salary and live in a comfortable cottage while my Japanese friends were working for $15 or $19 a month and living in great discomfort!

When I explained that we were Quakers, Nash became enthusiastic. He asked if I knew Charles Rhoads or Henry Scattergood of Philadelphia under whom he had worked in the Bureau of Indian Affairs during the Hoover administration. When I told him they were both my personal friends, he immediately shook my hand exclaiming, "Any friend of theirs is a friend of mine!" Then he dictated a letter to the secretary, saying to us in the meantime that if we could not join his staff, at least we should feel free to visit the camp as often as possible. The letter read:

To Whom It May Concern:

This will permit Mr. and Mrs. Herbert Nicholson and their three children to enter this camp at any time, and stay as long as they wish.
                          Roy Nash, Director
                          Mansanar Relocation Center

The contrast between Manzanar on our first visit and Manzanar a few months later was remarkable. Bleak and forbidding at first, the Japanese soon made it more livable. Every block had its flower garden, and an especially beautiful Japanese garden was planted and carefully tended in front of the hospital. A stunning stone guard house was built at the gate to the camp. Vegetables and melons and other garden produce were raised in abundance. I often took such things home with me as gifts after my visits to the camp. Unfortunately, not all the camps developed in this way.

Just before we left the camp on our first visit, Tom

Yamamoto, a grocery man from Terminal Island, gave me the pink registration slips for his pickup truck and for his one-and-a-half ton stake truck. He wanted them taken out of storage at the Japanese language school near Whittier. He asked me to sell the pickup, which was nearly new, and to load the stake truck with much of their furniture, as well as that of others, and to bring it all up to Manzanar the next time we came. I agreed to do it for him. Although I didn't realize it at the time, this was the beginning of my career as a truck driver.

Chapter 11

Truck Driver

I began my truck driving career by taking Tom Yamamoto's truck out of storage and loading it with his furniture and other belongings. I delivered the load to Manzanar and gave him the proceeds from the sale of his second truck. Then I returned to the language school in Whittier to get other things requested by those who had also stored their goods there. But when I arrived at the school the second time, I discovered that the place had been burned down and everything either stolen or destroyed! Unfortunately, such vandalism of the Japanese storage centers was not uncommon.

Since I could do nothing about the things that were lost, I decided to take the truck to West Los Angeles and load it with things stored at the church. Then I returned to Manzanar.

It was my third trip to the camp. When I arrived, Yamamoto took me aside and said that because I had rescued so many things and had saved his truck, he wanted to give me the truck! I was very touched by his offer, but I refused to take it outright. Instead, I consented to taking possession of the truck's pink registration slip with my name inserted as operator of the vehicle. That way I could continue to use it for helping the internees. It was a fine Dodge truck with only 25,000 miles on it. In the course of my travels, I added another 50,000 miles. The stories of my experiences with that truck would fill another book.

Each round trip to Manzanar was 500 miles. Poston and Gila camps were 1,000 miles. As I visited the camps, I took notes of the things people needed. Many Japanese also wrote us of their needs, so our mailbox was generally full.

My biggest job most of the time was to get things out of storage. If things were not well marked, or if everything was packed tightly together, it complicated matters a lot. Since the people had very little notice before moving out, most of the packing had been done in great haste without time for careful sorting and marking. If the springs wanted were the ones at the bottom of a high pile of items, or if the trunk requested was the bottom one in a pile of six, the task was formidable! Loading pianos was also a major job. My sons, Samuel and Donald, often helped me with the loading until Samuel went off to a conscientious objectors' civilian public service camp at Mammoth Lakes.

At times the things people in the camps requested had been stored with Caucasian friends. This occasionally created problems when the friends would not give me what was wanted without a written request from the owner. A couple of times I was told that the refrigerator or the piece of furniture needed had been given to them. They were using it and would not give it up! But most people were cooperative and sympathetic, wanting to know how their friends in camp were.

At first pets were not allowed in the camps, but when this ban was lifted, I transported many dogs and cats to their owners. One dog at Poston would always dash up to me and lick me because I had brought him out to his family. Once I even took a pedigreed cat from Manzanar to be treated in a pet hospital in Pasadena.

Because I was providing this trucking service, I was allocated plenty of gasoline. Even then, I could not possibly take everything requested out to the camps myself. Sometimes I had to take things to the Western Truck Lines and load them on one of their trucks going out to the camps. It was necessary for me to load everything onto the commercial trucks myself because the truck drivers were bitter against the Japanese and would deliberately damage or smash things.

The War Relocation Authority also sent men to places where internees had things stored, and they would take them to commercial truck lines to be delivered. This was done free of charge. Some of the Japanese thought that I was being paid by the WRA and did not cover my expenses. However, most of the people realized that I was not in the commercial trucking business and therefore could not charge for my services, so they would give me some money in an envelope.

Although most of the people we helped were genuinely appreciative, a number of times my work with the truck got me into serious trouble. For example, one day when I was at Manzanar, a nurseryman from West Los Angeles approached me and asked me to bring him a hidden treasure from under his house. He gave me explicit directions about where to dig for it. I went to the house and discovered some people were living in it. I figured that if I told them about the money, they might dig for it themselves and find it. So I went at night. While they were singing and making a lot of noise in the house, I sneaked into the yard and dug where I had been told to dig. But I found no treasure. The next time I was in Manzanar, I told the nurseryman what I had done, and he told me I had dug on the wrong side of the house! He meant for me to dig on the other side of the house, toward the street. I was foolish enough to go again, and, sure enough, I found a piece of pipe about four or five inches long with both ends soldered tight. Their "treasure" was in the pipe. I was certainly foolish to risk my life sneaking about the house in that way. I might have been shot, or a dog might have gotten me.

I put the pipe on the front seat of my truck and started for home. When I came to a stop light I put on the brake so hard that the pipe fell onto the floor. I reached down but could not find it, so I pulled over to the side of the road to make a thorough search of the car, the street, the gutter—-everywhere. To my great dismay I never did find that piece of pipe! What should I do?

The next time I was in Manzanar, I reported to the family exactly what had happened, but they would not believe me! They insisted that I give them the $150 they claimed they had stuffed into that pipe. Well, I just didn't have that kind of money, and those folks thought I was a liar and a thief.

At Christmastime Madeline and I received many monetary gifts and my good wife insisted that I take $150 to this family. When I gave them the money, all they said was, "We knew you were a liar!" They showed no recognition that I had risked my life for them.

Another time I sold a car belonging to a Manzanar couple who had not known us before the evacuation. I gave them all the money from the sale. But later the wife said that there had been an extra tire in the car, and they would like to have it back so they could sell it. I had to go to the person who had bought the car to see if I could get the tire. He told me that, knowing where the couple's things were stored, he had taken it to the West Los Angeles church and thrown it into the church storeroom. I went there but could not find it. Apparently more things had been thrown on top of it by other people.

Every time I went to Manzanar after that, this lady would get after me. Finally she took me to the authorities and demanded that I pay for the tire, believing that I had taken it out of storage, sold it, and pocketed the money! The official dealing with the situation knew that I was an honest man and tried to calm the lady down by urging me to take another look. Well, I finally did find the tire and took it to Manzanar. Again I was told I was a liar.

For the most part, however, my experiences with the truck helping the people in the camps were most positive. Recently I met a Nisei woman who told me that I had taken a crate of day-old chicks to her family when they were at Manzanar. She also remembered that I had taken her father, brothers, and sisters in the truck down to Hillcrest Sanatorium near Pasadena to see their mother before she died. She had been only eight years old at the time, but she still remembered this kindness. I had completely forgotten both incidents, and many others, but I am constantly reminded that there are those who do remember.

We used the truck not only for hauling people and personal goods back and forth between the camps and Los Angeles, but sometimes for other projects as well. Late in 1942 William Carr, a real estate man from Pasadena, and the Friends of the American Way, a Pasadena-based group of which we were both members, decided to send Christmas presents to the evacuees in the camps, especially Manzanar, Poston, and Gila. We had lists of the men, women, boys, and girls in the camps, and our goal was to send suitable presents for each one. No gift was to be more than a dollar in value.

My job was to go around to the various evangelical Christian churches and present the project. I am ashamed to say that not a single one of these churches or Sunday schools would support this endeavor for fear of "comforting the enemy." However, there were always a few individuals in each church who were willing to help us. I am grateful to be able to say that much. More liberal churches did cooperate.

The Pasadena First Methodist Church gave 5,000 gifts each year.

In early December of 1942, Manzanar reached a state of extreme unrest. Ralph Merritt, the new director of the camp, called in soldiers who, in panic, fired into the crowd. A teenage boy from Pasadena was killed. Another person died later. Because of the uproar the camp was closed to all visitors for some time. I was the first such person to be admitted after the trouble. I came in with my load of 10,000 Christmas presents. We held meetings and the Christmas spirit prevailed. There was no more violence.

I discovered that because of the unrest 70 ultrapatriotic internees and their families, with a few administration staff members, had been taken to an old Civilian Conservation Corps camp in Death Valley. I also had gifts for these people, so I received permission to go there. We had a wonderful Christmas party when I arrived. I felt that William Carr, who was really the man behind all these gifts, would have made a splendid Santa, but he always refused to go to the camps. He did not want any publicity.

One of the most memorable trips I made was when I took Roy Smith, a Methodist missionary who had been in Japan at the time of Pearl Harbor, to Manzanar to tell the people about how the war started there. Roy was in Kobe when the war broke out. Like other missionaries, he had been confined to his quarters as an enemy alien by the Japanese government. In August, 1942, he was allowed to return to the United States on the Red Cross exchange ship *Gripsholm*.

Practically the whole camp gathered in a mess hall and the space outside for this meeting. Mr. Merritt, the director, asked me to lead the meeting. When the preliminaries were over, Roy spoke in English, while an excellent interpreter relayed the message to those who needed Japanese.

Roy simply related how as he was shaving Monday morning, December 8 (Japan being on the other side of the International Date Line), a friend called to him that Pearl Harbor had just been bombed. Shocked, he ran out into the street —with half his face still under lather—to find out more. Later that day he went as usual to his classes at the Commercial University, but he soon had to stop teaching. He remained in his own home, was provided ration tickets and treated kindly by his Japanese friends.

On the whole, very few Americans were put into prison as enemy aliens. One exception was saintly Dr. H. S. Myers, the pastor of the Kobe Union Church. He was kept in solitary confinement because, as their pastor, he had had close association with the people in the American consular offices. But he held no bitterness or resentment against the Japanese for this.

When Japan's leaders learned that the Japanese in the United States had been confined *en masse* in concentration camps, they began holding Americans in mission school dormitories where they could be closely watched. Of course, the Japanese in America were not being held in concentration camps like Hitler's. Though the American camps fit the dictionary definition of concentration camps, and even Roosevelt used the term, they were not the systematic torture chambers that the Nazi death camps were. That does not mean there was no deprivation or that what happened in our country can be excused.

Roy Smith went on to tell the folks at Manzanar about how in the summer of 1942 the neutral Swedish ship *Gripsholm* was used for the first of two wartime exchanges of Japanese aliens for Americans who had been in Japan at the outset of the war. Some American missionaries on board had prepared a statement during their trip to give to the press about the treatment they had received under the Japanese government. When they arrived in New York they gave this statement to the reporters, but it was not accepted!

The report made clear the reasonable treatment they had received. They were told that nothing good about Japan would be reported in America.

The audience was so stirred by the message Smith gave that I felt it right to conclude with prayer in Japanese. It was a most successful meeting and did much to raise the spirit of the camp. Later I took Smith and another missionary, Howard Hannaford, to Poston where we had mass meetings in each of its three camps, and then to Gila for meetings in two camps there.

When I drove the truck out to the camps I seldom made the trips alone. There was always someone who wanted a ride. I usually had two passengers. It was a great help when one of my companions could share some of the driving. I welcomed opportunities to travel to camps other than Manzanar, Poston, or Gila. I went once each to Topaz in Utah and Minidoka in Idaho, twice to Heart Mountain in Wyoming, and several times to Amachi in Colorado. As a result, I believe I had a unique opportunity to get a wide, first-hand perspective about what was happening to the interned people.

Chapter 12

I Go To Jail

Throughout the war, I was asked to speak at churches, schools, and service clubs. I thought it best not to talk about the war itself, so I concentrated on what was happening to the American Japanese in the relocation camps and federal prisoner-of-war camps. I always made a point of asking the audience to write to Washington to protest, requesting that the internees be allowed to return to their homes. Often I would collect things donated for the people in the camps. In schools I usually talked about the cultural aspects of Japan that were admirable.

At service clubs I was often approached with, "Tell us the truth about this war. We know we are hearing only one side." I certainly was not in favor of the Japanese government, but I could talk about many things that were not known in our country. For instance, I could explain that the Emperor and Japan's ambassadors Kurusu and Nomura were innocent in the Pearl Harbor betrayal. The Japanese military machine had taken power into their own hands.

No service club where I spoke ever reported me to the FBI. But often when I spoke in churches someone would ask about Pearl Harbor and I would explain my viewpoint.

Later they would report me to the FBI. The FBI had to investigate every such report, of course, so I had several visits from them. Most of them were understanding, but one man told me I had better be careful or I would land in jail! I told him there were lots of men better than I already in jail. They were called "non-criminal criminals," in other words, conscientious objectors who numbered 5,000.

As a matter of fact, I did land in jail! It happened sometime later and it's quite a story.

Several times during the war, I was aked to get automobiles out of storage and drive them to their owners who had moved inland from the West Coast. On one such occasion I was to get a Buick that was being stored in Pasadena and to take it to Denver. It's really a job to get a car that has been stored for two years into running condition again, but I managed to get this one operating and reached Poston on the way without any trouble.

When I got to the camp, I met a man who was a recruiter for the frozen food industry at Seabrook Farms, New Jersey. He had come to Poston to find people in the camp who would volunteer to go to Seabrook as laborers. This arrangement was allowed by the War Relocation Authority, but the recruiter had not been very successful. The problem was that an agent from Seabrook who had been to Poston previously had misrepresented the work and the housing conditions at Seabrook. Some of the Japanese who went at that time had since returned to the camp disappointed. The arrangement was not an unfair one, but the misrepresentations had created false expectations.

The recruiter was now headed for the Gila camp. He asked if he could go with me since I was headed that way. I was always grateful for some company on the long trips, so I agreed. It later proved providential that I had let him come along.

Not far out of Poston, in the desert, the tubes carrying the brake fluid in the car crystalized. In order to unlock the brakes I had to break one of the tubes. Of course all the fluid ran out. The brakes loosened all right, but now we had no brakes at all!

I drove from there to Phoenix anyway—a couple of hundred miles! We simply had no choice but to go on. In order to stop the car, I would put it into low gear and then turn off the engine. It worked! When we reached Wickenberg, Arizona, about five in the afternoon, I telephoned ahead to the Buick place in Phoenix to ask if they could fix the brakes for us that night. They said they would if we could make it to town before they closed. We arrived about 8 p.m. Fortunately, they were still open.

While the car was being repaired, the Seabrook man and I went to a hotel where we shared a room for the night. I was surprised when I saw the man pick up the telephone and call his wife in Ventnor, New Jersey. He talked with her for half an hour! Then he suggested I talk with my wife, all charged to his company. I was grateful for his offer. After I talked a few minutes with Madeline, who was very surprised by the call, my new friend told me more about the situation he was in. Because the company was having such a hard time getting laborers to work for them, he offered me $50 for every man I sent them. To prove he was serious, he gave me an advance check of $50. I had been concerned about how to pay for the car's repairs, so the check was most welcome.

I subsequently managed to get quite a number of people from several camps to go to work for Seabrook, and most of them were satisfied with the situation they found there. If only that man had put into writing his offer of $50 per person! As it was, the first fifty was all I ever received.

I drove on alone from Gila to Denver. I arrived safely, delivered the car, and received $88 to cover the expense of getting the car there. The owner then loaned me his Ford runabout so I could drive out into the country to look up an Issei couple, the Tom Shinodas. When they had been at Poston, I had helped them move the furniture and clothing from their lovely home in Imperial Valley. They had lost all their property through government confiscation. Now they were farming in Colorado.

I was having a little difficulty finding them, so I stopped at a country store to ask the loungers out in front if they could tell me where there were any Japanese living in the area. A boy said he could show me a place. He hopped into the car beside me and we soon found a Japanese family. They were not the Shinodas, but by conversing with them a little in Japanese I was able to find out where my friends were living.

When we arrived at the place I was amazed. Their former home had been beautiful. Now they were living in what amounted to a shack. Nevertheless, I received a warm welcome and an invitation to breakfast the next morning. I returned to the store with the boy and then checked in at the neighboring motel. I soon was fast asleep, since it had been a long trip and I was very tired.

Suddenly I was rudely awakened, at about one in the morning, by a man holding a gun at my head. "There goes that $88," I thought to myself. But instead, the man showed me his sheriff's badge and ordered me to get up. I tried to tell him who I was, but he said that I had stolen money from the motel cash register and that I was a spy.

At the county jail they took everything away from me and then locked me in a sort of cage which contained three cells, each with two metal shelves that pulled down for beds. All the cells were empty, and the flush toilets in two had overflowed. I took a dirty army blanket from each of the cots and put them all on the one in the cleanest cell and soon was fast asleep again.

In the morning a fellow prisoner, a "trustee" who appeared to have a certain degree of freedom, brought me a tray with some oatmeal, coffee, and a roll. I didn't feel hungry, so I told him he could have it if he liked. As we talked, I discovered that he was an alcoholic who often came to the jail to sleep off a binge. His wife belonged to the Nazarene church. He told me that he had been to the mourner's bench about his problem several times. But he had not changed, and now his wife was going to divorce him. I suggested that we kneel right there and pray for God to help him.

In the middle of our prayer, the deputy sheriff came in. He swore at the man on his knees and kicked him. Then he let me out of my cell and took me to the sheriff.

I saw at once that the sheriff was a rather gruff sort of man. "Do you know why you have been brought in?" he asked.

"Yes." I had figured out that the boy who had gone with me to help me find the Japanese family was angry because I had refused to let him drive the car I was using. In revenge he had apparently reported me to the sheriff's office as a spy. The fact that I spoke Japanese probably gave him the idea. However, I didn't reveal my thoughts to the sheriff. Instead I said to him, "Last night I was confused and surprised, but now I understand it."

"Ah, your conscience is troubling you, is it?" was his reply.

"No," I said. "God sent me to jail to help that poor alcoholic, and to have a talk with you."

He scoffed at that. Then he began to question me thoroughly. I asked him to call the War Relocation Authority office in Denver to find out who I was. He swore at me and said, "Who's doing this investigation!"

When the sheriff was through with me, I was sent back to the jail for several hours of meditation. No food was offered me, though noon passed and I was getting hungry. At about

2 p.m. the sheriff sent for me again.

But what a change! This time when I walked into his office he said he was mighty happy to see me. Although he didn't apologize for his previous manner, he told me he wanted to know more about the Japanese. I could see that this man was like many others, essentially a good man who, because of the war, had been embittered against the Japanese. The treatment such men accorded the Japanese who had resettled inland was a reflection of this bitterness.

I told the sheriff that if he wanted to meet a real American, he should meet Tom Shinoda and his wife. I explained some of the things that his family had been through and the wonderfully patient attitude with which they had faced it all. The sheriff thanked me for giving him a new outlook on the whole situation, saying he would get acquainted with the Shinodas. Then he let me go.

Meanwhile the Shinodas, with whom I had promised to have breakfast, were wondering what in the world had happened to me! When I finally got to their home in the late afternoon, they were astonished at my story. After a good visit with them, I caught a late train out of Denver for the camp at Heart Mountain, Wyoming, the next stop on my way home.

About this time the Friends' Service Committee decided I was too dangerous to be going about for them, especially with all the speaking I was doing, and the preaching I did when I went to the camps. So our formal relations were terminated. This left me free to go about and speak as the Spirit moved me. There were no hard feelings in this decision, and I cooperated with the Service Committee on many occasions afterward.

1. Ernie, Artie and Herbie, Rochester, New York 1894

2. Madeline,
Cedar Rapids,
two years old

3. Village evangelism

4. Grandma Nicholson and Virginia in rickshaw, 1924

5. Our home in Higashi Hara, 1931

6. At our front gate at Higashi Hara

7. Shimamura (left) and one night's guests at tramp lodge, Higashi Hara

8. Funeral at Manzanar Relocation Center

9. Virginia, Samuel and Donald with parents, 1949

10. Shimamura and his two children at old folks' home

11. Five condemned murderers at Sapporo with Nicholsons and officials

12. Relief goat
leaving San Francisco

13. Presenting goats at Gotemba, 1948

14. Karuizawa home, 1961

15. Golden Wedding Anniversary, 1970

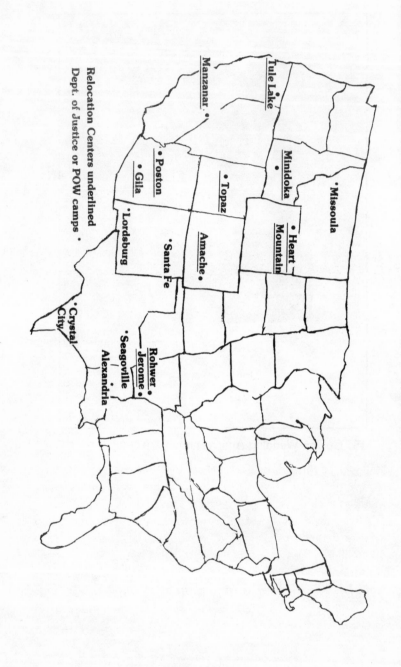

Relocation Centers underlined
Dept. of Justice or POW camps •

Tule Lake
Manzanar •
Poston •
Gila •
Topaz •
Minidoka •
Missoula •
Heart Mountain •
Lordsburg •
Santa Fe •
Amache •
Crystal City •
Seagoville •
Rohwer •
Jerome •
Alexandria

Chapter 13

Hillcrest

The smallest evacuation program from the official stand-point was actually the most significant one for us. That was the evacuation of some 156 patients with tuberculosis from Olive View and other sanatoria in the Los Angeles area to Hillcrest, a private sanatorium in La Crescenta. It was just 25 miles round-trip to Hillcrest from our home in Pasadena.

The sanatorium was actually a detention center under the WRA. It was guarded and no one could enter without a pass. The Olive View chaplain gave my wife and me passes to visit Wednesday and Sunday afternoons. Until the resumption of our work in Japan some eight years later, Madeline seldom missed visiting on these days.

At this time, Madeline learned to drive. I was often away on trips with the truck, so if Madeline was going to be able to visit Hillcrest regularly, we decided that she should drive. Although she was past 50 at the time, she managed very well. Each week she drove around town purchasing things the patients needed, often taking along Christine Jansen, a sweet Mennonite lady. Then on Sundays and Wednesdays they went to the sanatorium together.

There were times when my trips made it necessary for me

to take our car, but fortunately we had been loaned a second car for the duration by Mrs. Kay Hiraiwa, whose husband Tsumataro I had helped when he was sent to Missoula. The gas allowance for this car was only five gallons a month, so it was necessary to be very conservative in its use.

The sanatorium was so short of staff that all patients who could be up and about were given jobs such as passing trays or helping in the kitchen. Before long the whole place was well organized and functioning like one large, generally happy family. Madeline was adopted as "mother" for the family, and everyone loved Christine.

Other visitors to Hillcrest were Father Hugh Lavery and Sister Mary Esther who were Catholics, Reverend Bigelow, the chaplain from Olive View, and another missionary from Japan. The latter was a bit jealous of Madeline and tried to have her pass revoked on the grounds that there were no Quakers at Hillcrest. To that I replied, "There may not be any Quakers, but we have 156 friends!"

When Dr. Babcock at the sanatorium found out what was going on, he exclaimed, "Mrs. Nicholson does more good here than all the doctors, nurses, and preachers put together!" So Madeline kept her pass.

During the war I had charge of about 35 funerals or committal services for patients from Hillcrest and the relocation centers. Father Lavery would not conduct services if there was cremation, because it was forbidden by his church. Since the Japanese usually preferred cremation, I generally had the task for Christians and Buddhists alike.

The first death came before the general evacuation. It was Fred Nakamura, a Catholic. The last time I was with him, I asked if he would like me to pray. "Yes, I would," he responded, "but Father Lavery told me not to let the Nicholsons pray with me."

"That's all right, Fred," I told him. "Let's each just pray quietly in our hearts."

Later Father Lavery and I became good friends, and he often asked me to pray for his patients!

When Mrs. Ota, a wonderful Congregational Christian lady, died, both Father Lavery and I participated in the service. When I planned the service I asked him if he would like to say something and he agreed to. I also asked a Church of Christ pastor who had lived next door to the Otas if he would like to participate.

At the service this pastor said, "This dear lady was never immersed, but I'm sure she went straight up to heaven because of her faith."

Then Father Lavery said, "Mrs. Ota was never baptized with Holy Water, but I know she went to heaven because she suffered so."

I said I was not so much concerned about Mrs. Ota's soul because that was in God's hands, but I did know that to be with her in the sickroom was to be in heaven on earth.

There were three patients in each of the rooms at Hillcrest, and Mrs. Ota's two roommates had both become Christians because of her influence. Madeline and I were at her bedside when she passed away. She asked us to pray for her husband, her son and daughter, and for several young men who had worked at their wholesale market. It was just like her to be thinking of others, even in the last moments of her life. Then, her face shone and she looked away saying, *"Ureshi! Ureshi!"* (Happy! Happy!)

Madeline became very fond of Sister Mary Esther, although the sister tried hard to win Madeline to Catholicism. They had many discussions about the matter. After we had returned to Japan following the war, Sister Mary Esther wrote to Madeline, "We don't understand now, but when we both get to Heaven, we'll understand."

The sanatorium secretary used to call us whenever there were emergencies. One week when I was away Madeline was called to Hillcrest every evening. If someone was dying, the sanatorium would call us to come over for what they called "Protestant last rites."

On one of these occasions a young man was having a heavy hemorrhage and was not expected to live. Madeline stood by his bed and told him of the famous Japanese pacifist preacher and writer, Toyohiko Kagawa. In his book *Over the Death Line*, Kagawa tells how as a young man he promised God that he would be His man if God would heal him. God did, and now Kagawa was well known in both Japan and America as an evangelist. The dying young man to whom Madeline was telling the story made the same promise Kagawa had. He too was healed and is still living.

Another time we were called because a girl named Marjorie was dying. We got there just as the doctor was coming out of her room. "Is it all right for us to go in?" I asked.

The doctor replied, "Reverend, you believe in God. I don't. Medical science has done all it can, and she will be dead in fifteen minutes. I turn her over to you."

We went in. The girl did look like death. Madeline put her hand on Marjorie's brow and quietly prayed. The hemorrhage stopped and the girl recovered.

One evening the sanatorium called to say that Mr. Namiji Kayano, an Issei whom we knew well, had been taken to the general hospital in critical condition with bleeding stomach ulcers. We went right over to the hospital and found his room. He looked very pale from the loss of blood. A black resident physician was attending him. When we left the room he explained to us that Kayano's stomach was filling up with blood. After a period of time the blood would be vomited up. This happened about every two hours. If it continued, Kayano would be dead before morning unless he could be given transfusions.

That was the problem. The mission account in the hospital blood bank was at zero because all the blood was being given for soldiers. I asked the doctor to borrow blood at once and promised that the next morning I would bring in plenty of donors. With tears in his eyes, the doctor thanked me and said he would order the transfusions to begin immediately.

I telephoned Rev. Allan Hunter at once. He had a dozen or so conscientious objectors in his church, Hollywood Congregational, and I was sure he could persuade them to come over to the hospital to donate blood. He said it would be no problem, and to expect them all at the hospital by 8 a.m. the next morning. His conscientious objectors would not take a gun to shoot Japanese, but they would give their blood to save one!

I also filled my car with volunteers the next morning. I was 52 years old at the time, so when I said I wanted to donate my blood too, they said I was too old. But I persuaded them to let me give it anyway!

When I went to Kayano's room, I was pleased to see that his color was much better. He was very grateful when I told him I had given a pint of my blood to save his life. But when I went on to explain that Chirst had given *all* His blood to save his soul, Kayona looked at me and said suddenly, *"Ah, wakatta!"* (I understand!) In spite of the transfusions, the physicians were unable to get him back to strength for operating, and he died.

Besides being on call for emergencies at Hillcrest we were also in charge of Vesper services there on Sunday afternoons. My job was to arrange for ministers to come speak to the group. I often spoke at the services, as did Reverend Sozaburo Watanabe, who was one of the patients. I found that it was nearly impossible for me to get an evanglical minister to come to the sanatorium for these Vesper services. This was a great disappointment to me. Most of them refused on the grounds that they were afraid they would be "comforting the enemy"! That attitude I just could not understand.

Chapter 14

Opening the Camps

On September 16, 1940, Congress passed the Selective Service Act, authorizing the first peacetime draft of men for military service in American history. A year later, August 12, 1941, in view of a worsening world situation, it passed the Selective Service Extension Act by a very close vote. It lengthened the time of service for drafted men and permitted sending draftees overseas. During this time a number of Nisei were inducted into the Army. James Kitsuse of West Los Angeles Japanese Methodist Church was one of these.

In June, 1942, as part of the aftermath of Pearl Harbor, the Army stopped drafting Nisei and began registering them as 4-F, undesirable, or 4-C, enemy aliens. Naturally, the Nisei resented this very much. The Kibei and some Nisei already in the military were reclassified as 4-C and given discharges. Those left in were assigned to noncombatant duty, often KP and the like, and not sent overseas at first.

Eighteen months later, January 28, 1943, Secretary of War Henry Stimson announced, in part because of the many requests by American Japanese to serve their country, that the War Department would accept Nisei volunteers for the formation of a special combat unit. This unit became the famous 442nd.

The announcement requesting Nisei volunteers created significant turmoil on all sides. Predictably, those who took a racial view of the Japanese loudly criticized the War Department's decision. In the camps, the announcement was greeted by some as an opportunity to demonstrate that Japanese-American assurances of loyalty were more than just talk. To others the proposal was a further adding of insult to injury. They had already proved they were loyal to America by not resisting the evacuation. Having lost their homes and suffering a complete disruption of their lives, they were now being asked to volunteer or send their sons to get killed! In Hawaii where the Japanese had not been interned *en masse,* the response to the appeal for Nisei volunteers was overwhelming. In the relocation camps on the mainland, the response, for obvious reasons, was not as great.

The following January, 1944, the Army re-opened the Selective Service to Japanese-Americans. Nisei in the camps were then subject to compulsory draft. When Dillon Myer, director of the War Relocation Authority, came to Pasadena in February, those of us concerned about what was happening to the evacuated people arranged to meet with him at the Orange Grove Friends' meetinghouse. At that meeting I expressed my feelings about the draft. It was most certainly wrong, and I knew it was creating a lot of bitterness. If the Army felt it could draft the Nisei, then the people in the camps should be allowed to return home.

Myer replied that the Army was the only agency that could give such permission. The WRA was a civilian branch of the government and could not tell the Army what to do.

"Well, who *can* tell the Army what to do?" I asked.

"You can!" was the emphatic reply.

Since public opinion was an enormous factor in the whole matter, Mr. Myers explained that those of us who felt as we did should appeal to the Army about it. He advised me to go to Washington, D.C. to see John J. McCloy, the Assistant Secretary of War, who was responsible for decisions about the Japanese, and express our feelings directly on the matter.

As soon as I could make the arrangements I was on my way. I planned to make several stops on the trip, the first being at Poston. When I arrived at the relocation center I went, as I always did, to the barracks where the Ishii family lived. This was the family who had earlier been forced to liquidate the stock from their drug store on Terminal Island in only 48 hours. On this visit I met their son-in-law, a young man who had been a fisherman before being sent to Poston. When he heard that I was on my way to Washington to see McCloy, he asked me to go with him at once to another barracks where a crowd of Terminal Island Nisei were gathering to plan a riot in demonstration against the new draft order. Of course I went with him.

The group was angry and bitter. When I got a chance to make a statement I explained as best I could that rioting was not the answer. In fact, it could only make matters worse. I told them that I was on my way to appeal to the Army in Washington, and suggested that they send a telegram to Eleanor Roosevelt. Mrs. Roosevelt had visited the Poston camp previously and had made a favorable impression on everyone. The men found my suggestion agreeable and promised to postpone any further action until they heard from me in Washington. Wade Head, director of the camp, helped two leaders of the group compose a telegram which they sent to the President, to Assistant Secretary of War, John McCloy, and to Dillon Myer of the WRA. After the young men left his office, Head thanked me, saying that he and his staff felt something was about to happen but they were helpless to stop it.

From Poston I went to Gila. At this camp I again met with

some of the Nisei who were now subject to the draft. They felt about the same as the Poston group. Certainly the situation was very unfair. I explained to the men about the nature of my trip to Washington and urged them to write to McCloy and express their feelings. I could not stay long at Gila, but felt that at least I had given the men a sense of being able to *do* something about the situation they were in.

The next part of my trip took me to the United States Army Camp Shelby, the training site located near Hattiesburg, Mississippi, for the 442nd Combat Unit. The general public was not then and still is not aware that beginning in December, 1942, a good many volunteer Nisei fought valiantly in the China-Burma-India theater of operations.

This was not my first visit to Camp Shelby. I had been there the year before, in the summer of 1943, to visit my friend Jim Kitsuse who had been named one of the cadremen to organize the 442nd. The chaplain, a Southern Baptist, was very friendly and had asked me to speak at the Sunday chapel service. I spoke about the love of God, and many of the men thanked me afterward saying they had not heard about love since the war began.

Now, on my way to Washington, I had a second opportunity to visit the camp. I arrived in Hattiesburg about 11 p.m. on Friday, March 17, 1944. When I phoned Camp Shelby, Mike Masaoka, whom I knew from the Japanese American Citizens League, answered the phone. He sent a jeep to get me at once. Since he was on night duty, he let me have his bunk—a good surprise for the other boys when they found me in Mike's bunk the next morning!

Saturday night there was a dance in the gymnasium. Several busloads of Nisei girls came for the event from one of the Arkansas internment camps. A chaperone for the girls, Mrs. Sugiyama, whose husband was sick far away at Hillcrest, sat next to me. Since we had never met before, she said, "Are you *the* Mr. Nicholson?"

On the other side of me sat a colonel who was visiting various Army outfits, giving them points on their various merits. He told me that the 442nd was No. 1 in discipline, in the amount of victory bonds purchased, and in sports. This fine quality of behavior in training was later reflected on the battleground. The 442nd became the most decorated unit in the United States Army in World War II. It's casualty rate was the highest in all United States history. Their record of heroism more than proved what the Japanese Americans had been saying all along to the rest of the nation—that they were loyal to the United States and had been falsely accused!

I reached Washington, D.C. on March 20 and went at once to the Pentagon. On arrival I asked to see Colonel Lee, whom I had known in Japan when he was the language officer at the American Embassy in Tokyo. I was given a badge which said, "Escort Required," and was told to go into a waiting room.

Within minutes a major with graying hair entered the room with a big smile and an outstretched hand saying, "Hello, Nick!"

It was my old friend Major Stier of the Tokyo YMCA! He was to be my escort. He took me at once to Colonel Lee's office. I told Lee that Dillon Myer had sent me to see Undersecretary McCloy to talk about opening the relocation centers. Lee telephoned McCloy and secured an appointment for me.

I also mentioned that I would like to see the man in charge of drafting the Nisei. Since I had forty-five minutes before seeing McCloy, Stier took me to the office of a captain who happened to have an Irish name. This man told me about the letters that had come to him from the Nisei in the relocation centers. He showed me some that were pretty bad, from my point of view, with swear words talking about "your blankety-blank old army!"

Nevertheless, I said, "Captain, you're Irish, aren't you?"

"Yes," he answered.

"My father grew up in Ireland, so I'm pretty nearly Irish, too," I said. "If the government put us Irish behind barbed wire with men in towers armed with guns to shoot us if we tried to get out, and then ordered us to be drafted into their old army, what would we do?

"Well," he thought a minute, "we'd kick over the traces!"

"Now put yourself in their shoes and read one of those letters again," I suggested.

He did, and before long began to smile. "I have to admit these fellows have guts!" he said.

When I left the captain shook my hand and thanked me for helping him to understand the situation.

Upon entering McCloy's office, I discovered two colonels were also present. Both remained in the room throughout my interview. One was a gray-haired tough-looking militarist, Colonel William P. Scoby. He was the man McCloy had sent around to the relocation centers to get Nisei volunteers for the 442nd. The other was a middle-aged, gentlemanly looking man, Lieutenant Colonel Harrison A. Gerhardt.

I first reported on my visit to Camp Shelby. The men were delighted at what I told them. Then I expressed my concern about the drafting of men out of the relocation camps which were, in effect, prisons. McCloy agreed with my point of view, saying that if the men were to be drafted, they should also be free to return to their homes. There was absolutely no reason to keep the Japanese Americans penned up. The 442nd had proved that the Nisei were loyal, and the Department of Justice, in all of its investigations, had found absolutely no evidence of sabotage or espionage on the part of any Issei.

The only remaining problem was public opinion. Washington was constantly receiving letters from the West Coast

urging them not to allow the Japanese to return. The problem was that there were very few letters asking for the
Japanese to come back. The "anti" letters were often only
mimeographed sheets, obviously from organized pressure
groups, but every one had to be counted.

"Now if you can fill this basket on my desk with letters
wanting the Japanese to return," said McCloy, "we'll open
the camps!"

Before I left McCloy's office I asked whether the military
would do indescriminate bombing of Japan as they were doing in Germany. I expressed my deep concern about
Japan's civilian population and also asked if my home city
Mito was to be bombed. McCloy said that the emperor's
palace, Kyoto, some other cultural centers, and the crowded sections of the cities would not be bombed. He did not
know where Mito was so he spread out a large map of Japan
that had red crosses on it where the bombings were to take
place. Mito was not marked. I shook his hand, thanked him,
and left the room.

Colonel Scoby followed me out into the hall. When we
were out of earshot, he grabbed my arm and said, "When
we get to Japan we're going to send them all to hell!" I was
to remember those harsh words in the not-too-distant
future.

As soon as I could, I telegraphed William Carr in
Pasadena to tell him the news. I also contacted the Poston
camp. Then I went to Philadelphia to consult the American
Friends' Service Committee. Next, I asked the National
Council of Churches to contact church people on the West
Coast, requesting them to start writing letters. I explained
the situation, saying that if people sympathetic to the in-
carcerated Japanese were ever going to influence the Army,
the time was NOW!

On my way back to California I stopped at the Amache
camp in Colorado. At a meeting of the camp council, I sug-

gested that the Japanese prepare a mimeographed letter to
be sent to their Caucasion friends, enclosing three airmail
envelopes—one addressed to John McCloy, one to the
President, and one to Dillon Myer. The letters were to say
that the Japanese were wanted back by their friends as soon
as possible. The director of Amache agreed to write to all the
other camps recommending the same action. I then went to
three other camps to present the project.

Within four months some 150,000 letters reached
McCloy in Washington. He wrote to the Friends of the
American Way to say that Washington was satisfied that
public opinion favored the return of the Japanese. Since
Pasadena had sent so many letters favoring the return, he
asked the Friends of the American Way to be responsible for
receiving a Nisei girl from one of the camps to attend
Pasadena Junior College in September, 1944, as a sort of
test of public acceptance. Dr. John W. Harbeson, president
of the college and a staunch friend of the Nisei, polled the
faculty and students on the issue. The faculty was 98% in
favor of taking in such a student, and the student body
100%!

Esther Takei, whose brother had been killed in the
442nd, arrived from Amache camp in Colorado in time to
start school. Hugh Anderson, a Quaker and an officer in the
Friends of the American Way, offered to have her stay with
his family.

There was considerable furor in the community during the
first weeks, with frightening phone calls, cars parading by
the house, and hostile letters. But there were many en-
couragements, too. One Sunday morning, a GI who had
been wounded in the Orient hitchhiked to Pasadena from a
veterans' hospital in Monterey, several hundred miles away,
to tell Esther to "stick by her guns." Others sent letters of encouragement.

Gradually things calmed down. Esther was a bright girl

and a good dancer. She soon was very popular at school. Her acceptance did much to improve feelings about the return of the internees to their homes.

Chapter 15

The Return

In October of 1944, we were told by the WRA that the official opening of the camps would be January 2, 1945. The army failed to make a formal announcement of the opening, however, until December, 1944. The delay was caused primarily by politicians who had interfered and gotten the matter put off until after the national elections in November. Even before that, however, some 2,000 Nisei had already returned to the West Coast.

On December 18, 1944, the Supreme Court handed down its decision in the Mitsue Endo case, stating that citizens of Japanese descent could not continue to be held legally in the detention camps. Twenty-four hours before the Supreme Court ruling was announced, the Army revoked the mass evacuation orders.

I would like to repeat that Dillon Myer, head of the WRA, had agreed already in February, 1944, ten months earlier, that the camps should be opened and *all* internees allowed to go home. John McCloy, Assistant Secretary of War, had told me in March, 1944, that the only problem was the matter of public opinion. By July this was also settled and the camps might have been opened except for the interference of politicians. Once the elections were over, the way was clear. Thus the Supreme Court decision really had very little to do with the opening of the camps.

Early in January, 1945, I drove up to Manzanar in the truck. I spent a week trying to persuade those left there that they should begin to return to their homes. Most of the Issei were very afraid of what might happen to them. After a week, I succeeded in convincing twelve Issei men to return to Pasadena with me to size up the situation.

Three of the men I brought out of Manzanar were from West Los Angeles. That part of town was considered the most dangerous for the Japanese because of a veteran's hospital there. Also, the Douglas aircraft plant workers were supposedly very anti-Japanese. But since the men wanted to see about their homes and to go to the West Los Angeles Bank of America to look into starting accounts, we went anyway.

When we walked in the front door of the bank, the president came forward and greeted the three men most warmly, saying he was happy to have them back. Next we went to the police station. The chief was also cordial, promising the men there would be no trouble, but warning them to keep off the streets at night and to keep away from the veteran's hospital.

At lunch time Gisuke Sakamoto suggested that we go to Nick's place, which was next door to where he had had his market. Like all the other restaurants on the main street, a "No Japs!" sign stood in Nick's window. We decided to risk going in anyway, although the place was full of Douglas plant workers. Nick, who was in the rear cooking, saw us come in. He rushed out of the kitchen, threw his arms about Mr. Sakamoto and kissed him in Greek fashion, on both cheeks. He asked some of his other customers to move from their tables and had us sit down. Then he served us a full dinner "on the house."

Toward evening we went to the home of a Methodist pastor in West Los Angeles to see about a place where the men could spend the night. If the previous pastor, Rev. Crowder, had still been there he would have provided us lodging. But the new man was frightened and refused to help. So we went to a man with whom I had had dealings in the past, the manager of a boardinghouse for gardeners owned by Japanese. This man said he would be glad to keep one of the men as long as he could stay. William Katsuki at once volunteered. Before the rest of us left, the manager warned William saying, "Be careful of that Mexican across the street. He's sworn he'll kill the first Japanese he meets."

William looked across to where the man had pointed and exclaimed, "Why, I know him! I taught him how to garden!"

He walked across the street with a big smile on his face. The fellow ran up and embraced him saying, "William, I'm so happy to see you home!"

All twelve men found places where they could move in and help with gardens until they could get their own homes back. When I took them back to Manzanar, they gave such a good report that others began to apply for permission to return home. The next few months we were really busy trying to find places for everyone. I made many trips to Manzanar to haul furniture back again, now that the long internment, more than three years for some, was over.

Hostels were established to house folks while they were getting reestablished. The largest one was the Evergreen Hostel in Boyle Heights. The Friends' Service Committee took over a large building that had once been a school for Mexican children. Volunteers scrubbed and made the necessary repairs to make the place livable. All the while I was busy with my truck collecting furniture. As many as 150 people occupied this hostel.

After January, 1945, our family guest room was nearly always occupied by young people discharged from Hillcrest.

About this time Mr. Kojima, who had been a patient there, died. His wife, Ichi, said she would like to give the rest of her life caring for former patients of the sanatorium. So Friendship Home was started in Pasadena. It became an after-care home, licensed by the county, and could take as many as fifteen discharged patients at a time. Mrs. Kojima was a splendid manager and cook, and the home was most successful. After a number of years, she retired and others took over the work. For many years Paul Hashimoto, a former patient, ran Friendship Home. At age 81, Paul decided there was no more need for a home, so it was closed in 1976.

Finally, after months of work getting people home again, I returned the truck to Mr. Tom Yamamoto, who had opened the *Iida Shokai* (grocery store) in the Little Tokyo section of Los Angeles. That truck had been a tremendous help to many people. Parting with it was like parting with an old friend. We had been through a lot together.

Meanwhile, events had been moving swiftly in the Pacific. General Douglas MacArthur had retaken all of the Philippines by late February and the marines had taken Iwo Jima, about 700 miles south of Japan. The first night bombing of Tokyo and Yokohama, both with extremely large civilian populations, took place on March 8, 1945. I immediately wrote John McCloy in protest and received a polite reply saying that only military objectives were being bombed. This was not true!

On April 1, Admiral Nimitz had landed 100,000 soldiers and marines on Okinawa, the largest island in the Ryukyu chain southwest of Japan. The Japanese had been quickly driven to the southern end of the island and were completely overcome in June. From that time on, the American B-29 bombers and naval planes freely bombarded Japanese ports and cities continually.

President Roosevelt died unexpectedly in April, 1945. Harry S. Truman became the new president. By May 8,

1945, President Truman, Prime Minister Churchill, and Premier Stalin announced that Germany had surrendered unconditionally. In July a new kind of bomb which scientists had been working to perfect was successfully tested at Los Alamos, New Mexico. An invasion of Japan was already being planned, and Truman conferred with his advisors as to whether or not this new bomb should be used against Japan.

Japan had begun sending out feelers for a negotiated peace, but on July 29 Allied leaders meeting in Potsdam, Germany, agreed to hold out for an unconditional surrender. They warned Japan that unless it yielded on that basis it would face "utter destruction."

On August 1 my home town of Mito was subjected to bombing. Five days later, the United States dropped the first atomic bomb on Hiroshima, located on Japan's main island of Honshu. A single bomb destroyed approximately three-fifths of this metropolis of almost 350,000 people. Two days later Russia entered the war against Japan, invading Manchuria. The following day, August 9, the United States dropped another atomic bomb on Nagasaki, a seaport town of 240,000 people. The city was reduced to ruins.

Again I wrote McCloy a strong letter of protest. I also wrote to President Truman. (Both of these August 11, 1945, letters are in the appendix.) This time there were no replies. On August 10 Japan negotiated for peace and on August 15 capitulated to the Allied terms for surrender. The war was over and the war casualties on all sides ended, but at a terrible price. And, the Untied States became responsible for ushering in the age of nuclear warfare.

As a pacifist, I have always felt that my whole energy should be put into the work for peace. War is clearly evil. Killing and destruction have never solved the problems which cause enmity between nations. Sometimes it appears that a war has "solved" one problem, but then hatred and fighting break out somewhere else in an endless cycle that more fighting cannot break.

Hiroshima is the ultimate symbol of the most terrible aspect of war—the destruction and suffering of the innocent. Some 200,000 people died in that atomic blast; thousands of others suffered beyond belief. Hiroshima is the record for all history that the innocent and unarmed are pawns in the larger politico-military game. This has always been true of war, but never in such unmistakable horror.

In this country my wife and I continued to help the evacuees from the relocation centers return to their homes. I wish I could express how much we loved those dear people and how we went through dark waters with some. The church in West Los Angeles asked me to help again with the Nisei services. We continued to visit Hillcrest regularly. We attended many weddings and even performed the ceremony for some of our Hillcrest couples. One day each week we spent the day at Olive View where there were about 60 Japanese patients. Long Beach and Harbor hospitals had some 30 Japanese patients each, and we visited both hospitals about once a week also. We often went to Maryknoll Sanatorium, City of Hope, Los Angeles County Hospital, and Rancho Los Amigos. We kept in close touch with Friendship Home, finding jobs and homes for those staying there, so there would be room for others released from the sanatoria.

Thus our lives remained busy and fulfilled even after the evacuees had returned to their homes. But gradually, as the emergency in America faded, we began to look more and more toward returning to Japan, where the need was greater than ever in the aftermath of the war.

Chapter 16

Okinawa

At first our return to Japan as a family was not feasible, but not long after we began to feel our attention drawn to the needs of the people there an opportunity presented itself where we felt we could help. An organization called Heifers for Relief, sponsored by the Church of the Brethren, decided to accept my offer to raise money and take goats to war-torn Japan.

Milk was in desperately short supply overseas and the Japanese children were being severely affected by the shortage. Ordinarily the Heifer project sent only bred heifers to ravaged areas. In this case, goats answered the need more readily, so goats were sent for the first time in its history. Later they sent all sorts of farm animals to many countries and aided poor farmers in the United States as well.

When I received approval of the goat project I went to work. I raised a good part of the money and bought most of the goats myself. Then I gathered a little group of men to accompany me on the first trip. Sim Togasaki, a Nisei from San Francisco, wanted to come because he needed to make contacts in Japan for his importing business. Although he knew nothing about goats, he was a hard worker and a great help because he spoke fluent Japanese. Ted Roberts, a dairyman who had always been interested in the Japanese, and Paul McCracken, a goat expert, also came with us. Paul was a Quaker, too, so I was glad to have him along. My son Samuel also came. He took color slides everywhere which later were a great help in raising money for more goats.

In October, 1947, we arrived in San Francisco ready to load up for the trip when we found, to our great disappointment, that the Army had decided to send us to Okinawa rather than Japan! The following load would be scheduled for Japan. That disappointment was to become God's surprise for us. What lay ahead was a wonderful adventure.

The Army had built pens for our two hundred goats on the rear deck of the *Simon Benson*, a small liberty ship which was not in good shape. We had a rough trip across the Pacific and were very relieved when we reached Okinawa safely. Later we learned that on its next trip the ship had split open! It was easy to believe.

Our arrival in Okinawa was an unforgettable experience. The harbor at Naha was full of sunken ships. The city had been completely destroyed. We could only stare in shock and pity.

We received a warm welcome and were greeted by the governor and other dignitaries. It was a delight to discover that Mr. Shikiya, the governor, was a Christian. After the ceremonies, in which we presented a goat to the community, we milked the remainder of our goats and took the milk to an orphanage.

We discovered that we were to be housed at the Military Government Headquarters across the island from Naha. Our escort there was a former missionary to Japan, Everett Thompson, who was in charge of LARA (Licensed Agencies for Relief in Asia). The occupation forces did not want to work with a lot of separate relief organizations, so they formed this agency to coordinate all relief efforts. The Heifer project joined LARA, as did the Church World Service, the Friends' Service Committee, and many others.

At the Military Government Headquarters we were taken to the officers' quarters. What a surprise to discover that we goatherds were classed as colonels!

The next morning we were taken to the office of Colonel Craig, a soft-spoken Southerner who was most cordial. When I asked if it would be all right for me to preach in Japanese while on the island, a lieutenant, who was also present during our interview, blurted out, "No! You're goatherds!" But Colonel Craig said it was all right as long as I didn't try to make Quakers out of everyone.

So we began. We went first to the north with a truckload of goats for a government stock farm and a hospital. We also had goats for several villages and for the Airakuen Leprosarium. At the leprosarium we held a meeting for all the patients. There I met Keya Aoki for the first time. He was a Christian patient who had come from Miss Riddell's leprosarium in Kumamoto, Japan, and now was the head of the church at Airakuen. Over the years we met again many times and became good friends.

We worked hard and the days passed quickly. By the time we finished our work, we had visited nearly every village on the island with a goat and a message. One evening Samuel said to me, "Dad, you talked six and a half hours today to a total of over six thousand people!"

Practically all of these talks were out of doors without a loudspeaker. The need to shout was tiring to say the least. Twice I spoke at a prison to about four hundred teenage boys and girls who had been given six month terms for selling cigarettes they had received from American soldiers. Another time Togasaki and I were asked to speak to some six hundred laborers in a quonset hut. The acoustics were terrible so that the men couldn't hear Sim. I decided to try. I had been speaking all day out of doors, but I prayed for strength, and God enabled me to hold that crowd spell-bound for nearly an hour. When it was over, Sim remarked, "Nick, you spoke better Japanese than you know!"

Everywhere the message we gave was essentially the same. I felt that more important than the goats themselves was the message they brought with them. They represented the loving sympathy of Christians in America. Also, like the goats of the Old Testament, they were a "sin offering." Everywhere we went I asked that America and Japan be forgiven for the suffering they had caused among the Okinawans.

The condition of the people was appalling. One-quarter of the civilian population had been killed or was missing, homes and cane fields destroyed. A great deal of it was wanton destruction. People were living in huts made with whatever scraps of material they could find. Most had practically no clothing other than the relief goods given to them. They had no food, no matches, no electricity, no light. The staple food was sweet potatoes. We had cold, boiled sweet potatoes for almost every meal. Fortunately, at the officer's barracks we always had a good breakfast.

At most of the meetings, when I asked the people to forgive us, someone in the audience would stand up and say that the Okinawans, too, needed to be forgiven for their misdeeds. It made a wonderful opportunity to tell about God's love in providing the "Lamb of God," Jesus Christ, as the wonderful "sin offering" for the *whole* world.

During our stay on the island I had to go to Colonel Craig several times to get help for Okinawans who had been mistreated by GIs. We did meet some splendid Christians among the GIs, but most of the soldiers exhibited disgraceful behavior. They got drunk and did all sorts of evil things. Stealing was rampant; it was called "scrounging." What's more, the GIs were encouraging the Okinawans to do the same.

One Nisei construction worker told Togasaki that besides their good salary he and the other workers got much more in "gravy." This fellow said that only one of them was really keeping straight. That was our Hillcrest young man who had been miraculously healed, Harold Tamashiro.

Harold's story is an unusual one. On the day before Pearl Harbor he had been admitted to the Los Angeles General Hospital with an advanced case of fistula and the X-rays of his lungs were clouded. The next morning he heard the newsboy in the hall calling, "EXTRA! EXTRA!" It was about the bombing of Pearl Harbor. Everyone in the hospital was shocked, of course.

Gradually Harold became aware that people in the ward with him were becoming uneasy at his presence because he was a Japanese. He could feel an invisible wall separate him from everyone else. The nurses were very kind and told the other patients that he was an American just like the rest of them, but the wall remained.

About two weeks later Harold become so desperately ill that he required surgery. Following the operation he was placed in an intensive care cubicle. He had lost so much blood from the surgery that he was unable to move. His temperature soared to 104 degrees. The nurses came in every fifteen minutes to check on him. They also had to feed him as he was too weak to lift a spoon.

The day before his birthday, December 20, some teenagers came to the hospital to sing Christmas carols to the patients. Harold was too sick to receive visitors, but the young people stood in the hall and sang for him. The music touched him deeply. He was in desperate straits. He felt that he might not live another day, not even long enough to celebrate his birthday. He decided to pray.

At that time he knew only vaguely that God existed and had no personal faith of his own. It is surprising to him now, years later, that he was even able to pray at all. This is what he prayed.

> *Dear God, tomorrow is my birthday, which should be the happiest day of my life, but I'm a sick man. I don't know if I'll live to celebrate it. It is you, God, who knows my future. If you believe that my time has come, please accept me. If you believe I have a future, give me back my health and I will do something for you.*

When he finished the prayer Harold fell sound asleep, without any pain.

During the night, he wakened suddenly. As he tells it:

> I heard a noise, quite loud. There was thunder and lightning. When I looked around I saw a tidal wave coming toward me. I wanted to run away, but there was nowhere I could go, so I closed my eyes and folded my hands. When I opened my eyes I saw a thread of light. I thought it might be a path, so I followed it. I was perspiring heavily, so I sat down to rest under a fig tree.
>
> When I looked behind me, I could see the tidal wave coming. When I looked down I saw that the land had fallen away, even under the tree, so that only the roots were left. There was a deep chasm there, so deep you could not see the bottom. A little smoke was coming up from it. I jumped back from the edge.
>
> Then I saw a man coming out of the wave. He was dressed like a fisherman wearing something like a Japanese *happi* coat with a rope for a belt.
>
> "Don't go over the bridge beyond," he said.
>
> I saw the bridge there, so I said, "Thank you very much."
>
> When the man turned away from me, I saw that

his profile was the profile of Jesus. Then he disappeared. I pinched myself to be sure I was awake. It was painful, so I knew I wasn't sleeping. I realized that Jesus had come to save me.

When Harold woke up in the morning the nurse on duty said to him, "Your temperature is going down!"

Every time they came to check, it had dropped another degree. By breakfast it was only 99 degrees! When his tray was brought to him, Harold ate everything up before the nurse could come to feed him. When she got there she could hardly believe that he had fed himself. Harold was celebrating his birthday after all!

About a month or so later all the Japanese TB patients at the community hospital were interned at Hillcrest Sanatorium. There he met Madeline and me and became part of the Hillcrest family. While he was there he had another severe hemorrhage. Madeline prayed for him and he recovered.

Then on March 28, 1944 he had another dream. This time he saw an island in a tropical region. There were banana trees and houses with thatched roofs. In his dream he was following a path as it twisted and turned. Suddenly he came to a place where straight ahead there was a little hill with a small park or gathering place for the village people. A woman was coming toward him. She was wearing black clothing and had a kerchief on her head. She was not Japanese. To Harold she looked like the lady who came regularly to Hillcrest, Christine Jansen. The woman did not speak to him, however. As she passed, he saw she was wearing a cross. Then she disappeared.

When Harold woke up and thought about his dream, he knew that it had not taken place in America since we have no banana trees or thatched roof houses here. His mother was living in Okinawa at that time, so he realized it must have been some place like that. But he still did not know exactly what the dream meant.

Almost one year after the dream, April 1, 1945, Okinawa was invaded by American forces. During that year, Harold had been discharged from Hillcrest, and as soon as Japanese were allowed to return to the city, he went back to school. When he finished, he applied for a job with the Atkinson and Jones Construction Company. He passed all the screening tests in spite of his previous illness, and got a job as an interpreter. The company sent him to work in Okinawa.

When he arrived on the island, Harold recognized the vegetation as being the same as in his dream. The first thing he wanted to do was to find the place he had seen in the vision. The search took him nearly a year, but he found the spot.

During his time on Okinawa, Harold met Clifford Schneider, an Army engineer from Little Rock, Arkansas. Clifford was a Christian and very interested in starting a Sunday school for the Okinawan children. He came to Harold about it, because he knew Harold spoke Japanese. When Harold told him about the site he had seen in his dream, they felt that they should make a start.

An old storage house was their first church. Later, people of the village gave them a piece of land—the place of Harold's dream! The spot was an open lot, ideal for a church.

A number of friends chipped in a few dollars. Money was collected every week and the lumber bought bit by bit. Building materials were very scarce, of course. The village people contributed the labor. With the labor donated, the task was completed in two years for about fifteen hundred dollars.

In February, 1953, I spent a month in Okinawa speaking in most of the schools and churches. Harold was still there some six years after my first goat trip. I visited his little church and preached to the villagers who gathered to hear me. I was "Uncle Goat" to them. The church is still there today.

So, although at first we were disappointed at not going to Japan with our load of goats, when it was all over we were grateful we had come! We had been drawn close to the Okinawan people and been inspired by them in many wonderful experiences.

Nevertheless, we still had a desire to go to Japan. When our work in Okinawa was over, we came home on an Army transport ship. Soon we were on the road again, buying goats, showing slides and talking about our experiences. In May of 1948 we were ready to start out again, this time for Japan!

Chapter 17

Uncle Goat

We sailed for Japan on the *Flying Scud* with two hundred fifty goats. Dick Clark, an expert photographer, was on board with color movie film to record the trip. When it was over he edited some two thousand feet of film into "*Ambaassadors of Peace*," the record of our trip with the emphasis on "baa." Besides Dick and his camera there was Al Brower, a ventriloquist with his doll Bill, Les Yoder, a Mennonite young man who came along to help, and Ty Nagano, a Nisei.

We sailed in May, which happened to be kidding time. We started out with two hundred fifty goats and landed with two hundred sixty-five! Just before we reached Yokohama, I was called from bed in the middle of the night. There was trouble in the maternity ward. I found "Temperance," given by the Women's Christian Temperance Union, in agony. She was having a breech delivery. Everyone was standing around not knowing what to do, so I rolled up my sleeves to help. I managed to get hold of the kid's legs and pulled while Temperance pushed, and out came a beautiful large doe. We named her Kiyoko, which means "purity."

When we landed in Yokohama, there was a welcome

meeting for us. On that occasion, I told the story of a young Nisei girl, Satomi Yasui, and her family in America who had raised four goats for our project. The Japanese Vice-Minister of Agriculture who was present at the meeting told me afterward that I should tell the story over the radio for the children's hour. So I went to the NHK (Japanese Broadcasting Company) office in Tokyo, but I was told that getting clearance for me to speak on the air would take six months.

Instead, I told the story to a newsman, a reporter for the women's hour, and to a young man for the children's hour. The young man elaborated on my story in his talk over the air. Another man heard the program and wrote it down for a large children's magazine, adding even more changes. Finally, with more additions, the story was put into a fifth grade reader, and I became known as "Uncle Goat."

In the reader, the story was no longer about Satomi, but about a boy named Harry whose father had been killed in the war with Japan. It was a very touching story about the sympathetic love of a lad who sacrificed to send a goat to the children of the man who had killed his father. In later years the printing of that story in the reader opened the way for me to speak in many schools all over Japan where I might otherwise never have had an opportunity.

Naturally I was very anxious to visit my old hometown of Mito. When we arrived we found that eight-five percent of the town had been destroyed in the war. The brick meetinghouse was just a shell. Ryumei Yamano, whom we had known in our early days in Mito, was now a leader in the Mito meeting. He very graciously invited us to stay in his home. Since he was an English teacher, he was acting as interpreter for members of the occupation. He told us many stories about how things were going.

For example, he said that an agricultural expert from the occupation forces had come to Ibaraki Ken and insisted that the farmers cut down some of their trees and plant grain. The farmers objected, saying that generations of farming had taught them that they must keep a certain portion of their land in trees to prevent flooding. The American replied that such belief was superstition. He ordered them to cut down the trees. The following spring, flood waters covered much of Ibaraki Ken.

Our former home, Higashi Hara, situated on a provincial road just out of Mito, I found filled with people. There was a whole family in every room! The old folks' home was also filled with refugees. During the fighting four incendiary bombs had hit our home, but none had caught fire. Eight hit the old folks' home. One had caught fire, but Shimamura had put it out with *futon* (quilts). Our lovely kindergarten and coworker's house had been completely burned.

The old folks' home needed help. It had fallen into disrepair and there was no one to help pay the running expenses. Mr. Tomita, a businessman whose children in earlier years had been helped by our goat's milk, came to the rescue and promised to pay the expenses and to oversee things somewhat until I returned to Japan. Also, during the war our Susumu Yamaguchi had helped a barber rescue his barber's chair. In gratitude, this man went for years to the old folks' home weekly to cut hair and shave the old men free. So it looked like things were going to start again.

After my visit to Mito I was anxious to return to America because I wanted to be there in time to send off the next shipment of goats. I found that if you contact the right people the impossible can sometimes be accomplished! The impossible in this case was to get my travel orders changed from ship transport to plane. Everything worked out fine and I soon found myself settled on an Army transport plane bound for home.

At Honolulu I was "bumped off" the flight for someone of higher priority. It was four days before I could get another

flight, so I used that time to tell the people in Hawaii about
the goat project. The Okinawans living in Hawaii sent me a
total of $35,000 for goats as a result of that visit. With the
money Heifers for Relief was able to send over five thousand
goats to both Japan and Okinawa. After four wonderful
days I made it back to San Francisco just in time to help send
off the next load of goats.

Of course, as soon as I was back in the United States, I
was busy speaking and raising money for the goat project.
On one of my trips to Oregon I visited Les Yoder who had
gone with me on the first trip to Japan with goats. On Sunday I spoke in the Mennonite church where he was a
member. After I left, one of the elders of the church
deposited six hundred dollars with the Japan Bible Society
so that Bibles could be furnished along with the goats.
Because of this gift we were able to give the recipients of the
goats post cards addressed to the Bible Society. If they
wished to have a Bible which would explain why Christians
wanted to help them, they could send in the card and a Bible would be sent to them free of charge.

In January 1949, after several strenuous months buying
goats, raising money and sending a couple of loads of goats
off to Japan, I was again in charge of another shipment. Les
Yoder was along again. In spite of a history of dreadful
seasickness, he was always ready for another trip. And what
a worker he was, even when sick! Narumi Hatayama, a
hard-working farmer from near Fresno, came along, and
also Korky Kawasaki, who had been with the Friends' Service Committee in Chicago. Korky came as our photographer, not that he didn't do his share of other work as well!

One of the most important places we went on our mission
for peace this time was Hiroshima. At Hiroshima I went to
both the governor and the mayor, and on behalf of the
Americans who felt ashamed for what our nation had done
to their city, I asked them to forgive us.

While we were in Hiroshima I was invited to speak in the Christian church where Reverend Kiyoshi Tanimoto was pastor. Reverend Tanimoto was one of the principal characters in the famous book *Hiroshima* by John Hersey. In his book Mr. Hersey describes vividly the horrors of the atomic blast and the terrible destruction that took place. At the church I asked the congregation to forgive us. The assistant pastor (Reverend Tanimoto was in America at the time of my visit) said in response, "On the other hand, forgive Japan for what she has done to you."

The large gathering rose as I prayed that God might forgive us all for our many sins against Him. The Holy Spirit fell on us, binding us together in the warmth of God's love.

It is hard for me to express the sadness I feel when people tell me I had no business apologizing to the people of Hiroshima. When they say that the bomb was justified because it saved millions of lives they do not know that Japan was already attempting to negotiate for peace through diplomatic channels days before the atomic bomb was dropped.

Recently when I spoke in a Japanese church in America, I told the story of my first visit to Hiroshima after the war. After the service, a member of the congregation told me that he had been outside the city of Hiroshima when the bomb fell. Many of his relatives and friends were killed or horribly burned. The days of clearing up after the terrible holocaust were tragic.

"I can't understand how Christians can justify that criminal act," he said. "You are the first American I have ever heard apologize!"

Now that I had completed three goat trips, two to Japan and one to Okinawa, and the goat project was pretty much operating on its own, Madeline and I began to look around to see if there might be some way that we could return to Japan to live.

The year was 1950. We visited groups of Quaker friends on the East Coast whom we had known through the years, hoping to find continuing support for future work in Japan. The New Jersey Friends guaranteed partial support, but in order to secure our visas, we had to be able to guarantee full support. We decided to return home to Pasadena and wait to see what might develop.

Soon after our return to California, we heard Norman Grubb of the Worldwide Evangelism Crusade speak. We invited him to visit us in our home. When he came, we spent a couple of hours talking, praying and thoroughly enjoying each other. Grubb invited us to help WEC get established in Japan. He offered to give us a letter that would assure us visas, since we would be going under their support. We agreed, and then spent the next few months in WEC training centers around the country getting acquainted with the organization and its people. By spring we were ready to go to Japan.

When the Japanese in Los Angeles heard that we were returning to Japan, the Chamber of Commerce in Little Tokyo invited us to a banquet in our honor. They presented us with a beautiful framed tribute to our work and a check for four thousand dollars! This gesture of appreciation touched us deeply. We used the money to buy our tickets on a freighter to Japan, for a movie projector, and for relief supplies. When everything was ready, we drove up to Oakland were we lived for a few days at the Home of Peace, a Christian home where missionaries stay while preparing to sail for the Orient. The folks there were a tremendous help to us in purchasing supplies, packing them, and getting them to the freighter on which we were sailing. We also visited congregations in the Japanese-American churches in the San Franciso Bay area while preparing to leave.

Our family was beginning to divide up. Virginia had already left for her first term as a missionary with the

Ramabai Mukti Mission in India. Donald was coming with us to help with the work. We were sorry that Samuel couldn't come too, but he was in college at the time. Of course he came to see us off and then drove our car back to Pasadena. In ten years we had driven that Chevy 181,000 miles, and it was still going strong. We hated to give it up!

At last we were on our way! Our hearts had yearned to return to Japan for years, and now it was finally happening. When we arrived we decided to make our old summer cottage at Karuizawa our headquarters. From there we could visit friends in Mito, Tokyo, Kyoto, and other places. Always we took gifts of food, vitamins, and clothing. We continually had our eyes open for a place for WEC to establish its headquarters.

We travelled for six months all over Japan trying to find the right place for WEC. At Ibusuki in Kagoshima where I had met Reverend Misaki Shimadzu on one of my goat trips to Japan, we visited him and his people again. Reverend Shimadzu wanted to change that hot springs resort town into a Christian town and asked us to come help him. One time a Christian from an island off Nagasaki came to see us and actually pled for us to come there. But we felt that neither place was ideal for WEC to begin because they were both very isolated. We also had invitations from other places.

Finally we went to Omi-Hachiman to visit the Omi Brotherhood. Because Omi-Hachiman was in the center of Japan, it seemed a more likely starting place for WEC. We had not gone there first because we knew that the Brotherhood felt they could handle their area by themselves. However, since we were close friends, one of their preachers took us to Gokanosho, a village where there was no church. We found a large mansion there for sale, perfect for missionary families. Right next to it was a large building that would be ideal for meetings, Sunday school, or even for a Bible school.

Then we were taken to another section of the village where there was a large house which had its second floor made into a separate apartment with a flush toilet. We rented the apartment for ourselves and sent word to WEC that we had found a place. Then we returned to Karuizawa, packed up and moved to Gokanosho. A new era had begun in our lives in Japan.

Chapter 18

Last Years In Japan

By the end of November, 1950, the first WEC couple arrived with their two small children. They lived with us in Gokanosho for about a month until they were able to acquire a house. Other WEC arrivals soon followed to start the Christian Literature Crusade work. We helped them all find places to live, and a place for the publishing work to begin as well. I had the honor of being father of the bride on two separate occasions when there were weddings among the WEC staff.

As WEC became established we gradually began to turn our attention to other avenues of service, particularly the one which we felt was really our calling—visiting prisoners in the penitentiaries and the sick in the many sanatoria and leprosaria. From Gokanosho we rode our bicycles on the country roads to the Omi Brotherhood sanatorium in Hachiman and to other nearby hospitals, including the national TB sanatorium just outside Yokkaichi, where we made many contacts. When we were in Karuizawa we visited the Kusatsu Leprosarium and the Nagano Prefecture sanatoria and prisons. I also travelled to more distant sanatoria, hospitals, and penitentiaries, always taking along my projector.

In addition, we kept up an extensive correspondence. I wrote an article each month for a little paper, the *Yo No Hikari* (Light of the World), which was being produced for sick folks by a friend of ours, Nobuhiko Naka. We received many letters in response which kept Fumiko Takenaka, my invaluable secretary, and me very busy. Fumiko was a lovely Christian girl who lived nearby and had been introduced to us by our landlord. She soon became like one of our own family.

Madeline and I continued a very busy schedule of correspondence and visitation until the summer of 1951 when I developed a thrombosis in my right foot. We were in Karuizawa at the time. A Japanese doctor diagnosed my problem and told me that my heart had been made in the Meiji era and that I should not put on Showa speed. That means my heart was of nineteenth century vintage and I should not act like it was made in the twentieth century!

I was ordered off my foot for six months. Medicine was prescribed by Dr. Joe Henry, along with certain simple exercises. For the first time in my life I was really restricted and had plenty of time for reflection and for the piles of correspondence that were always waiting.

We set up a little schedule. At 8 a.m. Donald went to the post office for the mail. Fumiko would arrive at 8:30. She read the letters and I dictated answers. Then we would do up packages of books and clothing that were to be mailed out. At noon Fumiko went to another room to eat her lunch and write the Japanese letters on which she had taken notes. I would have a rest and then would work on the English letters until she came back to read me what had been written in Japanese. Donald would then take the letters and packages to the post office for the outgoing mail.

I don't know what we would have done without Donald.

Besides acting as postal carrier, he accompanied Madeline when she visited the local hospitals. They almost always went by bicycle. One day they rode over 30 miles. Madeline was past sixty at the time!

During this time, Merrell Vories of the Omi Brotherhood cabled our son Samuel asking him to come to Japan to teach English in the Brotherhood's school and several near-by government schools. He came, and it was wonderful to have him nearby so we could see him often. He stayed for four years teaching English and holding Bible classes.

In October, 1951, after being confined to bed for two months, I received a letter from a young Nisei woman who was attending a Bible school in Missouri. It contained a handkerchief over which an evangelist had prayed. One Sunday, while the others were at church, I put the hankie over my foot and spent the time in prayer. Of course, I continued the doctor's instructions also. Then on New Year's Day another Japanese doctor visited us and examined my foot. He asked me if I had ever used tobacco. I told him, "No."

"You're lucky," he said. "The chances are you would have had to have your leg amputated had your bloodstream been weakened by nicotine."

I told him it wasn't luck, but plain common sense. We thanked God and I continued to be careful until the foot was completely well.

When I was able, we continued our visitations. During this time our only regular income was $50 a month, sent to us by our faithful New Jersey Friends. This amount covered our normal living expenses. God fully supplied all our other needs. Gradually our trips to the many TB sanatoria from Hokkaido to Okinawa came to include all ten government leprosaria as well. The heads of these institutions always received us warmly. We became friends with many of the doctors and nurses, as well as with the patients. It is remarkable how many of the staff we met were Christians or favorable to our message.

Some of the doctors we met became especially dear to us. Dr. Kensuke Mitsuda, head of the Nagashima Aiseien Leprosarium in Okayama, was internationally known as a specialist in leprosy. The first time we visited his institution this kind doctor had a banquet prepared for us! He was not a Christian, but he recognized the value of the Christian members of his staff. Later he was baptized a Catholic, and I prayed at his bedside when he was dying.

Dr. Saikawa, also of Aiseien, was another of those to whom we became close. We were able to help him make arrangements to visit India and spend time working at the famous leprosarium at Vellore. Eventually he went as a missionary doctor to Taiwan where he also worked with the World Health Organization. Later he became director of the Leprosarium in Okinawa.

Dr. Miyazaki, an earnest Christian, head of the leprosarium at Kumamoto, was deeply interested in India. Service Clubs of Japan sent him there to investigate the possibility of opening a leprosarium. During his visit he met Prime Minister Pandit Nehru who gave him 100 acres of land at Agra for such a project. In 1964, a leprosarium was established there in sight of the Taj Mahal. After Dr. Miyazaki was killed in a plane crash, another Japanese Christian doctor and a staff of thirteen Japanese nurses carried on his work.

I have lost track of how many TB sanatoria we visited during that time. But I'll never forget Seiranso Sanatorium in Ibaraki Ken. Dr. Yasuyuki Kano saw me one day in the wards and asked me to stop in at his house when I had finished. He was a very important man, one of the leading chest surgeons in all Japan. That evening as we talked, he told me that he was not a Christian. But then he walked over to a bookshelf and took down a New Testament, saying,

"Before I go into surgery I always take this book and read one of the miracles of Jesus. Then I go into the operating room with a power beyond myself."

The most precious of our experiences during those years of visitation was when we met Fusa Shina, a Christian patient at Tohoku Leprosarium, north of Sendai. Because of the dread disease she had contracted, this woman had been separated from her family and shunned by society. Her face and limbs were terribly defaced by the disease. Nevertheless, day after day, holding her pen between the stubs of her thumb and forefinger, she wrote letters of encouragement and faith to many others in distant places.

As a result of this woman's witness, as many at 40% of the patients in the leprosarium became church members. Through her letters to patients in another sanatorium, a Bible study class was started. Once we gave her the name of a young man in a penitentiary in Shiga Prefecture. Through her correspondence, this young man was led to Christ. Many evangelists and ministers of the Gospel, even some as far away as Hawaii, also received encouragement and inspiration from her letters. In spite of her own great suffering, especially during the cold winters when the pain was severe, she always carried the attitude of victory. It was a great privilege to have known this wonderful woman.

Prisons were also a part of our visitations. Another of our thrilling experiences during this time was with the Calvary Society, started by Matao Uchida. The Calvary Society was made up entirely of convicts on death row in the various penitentiaries in Japan. Uchida himself had killed two people. While he was awaiting trial, he began to read the Bible. Through this experience he was converted.

Uchida wanted to share what he had discovered in his newfound faith with other men waiting execution on death row throughout Japan. Fortunately, he had been granted permission to write as many letters as he wished during his imprisonment. He felt that since Christ had won only 50% of the men on the cross with him, he should not set his goal any higher. At that time there were 70 murderers awaiting execution in Japan. His goal was to win 35 of them to the Lord. Through his efforts half of the 70 did accept Christ! I was able to visit and pray with most of these men. In spite of all we tried to do to influence the authorities on behalf of this very special man, Uchida was hung some years later.

Very recently in California the death penalty was put to a popular vote. People were emotionally upset because there had been some horrible murders. The death penalty was restored by a great majority of votes, in spite of an earlier Supreme Court ruling that capital punishment was a form of "cruel and unusual" punishment and thus unconstitutional. I must admit that it is a topic about which I am also emotionally stirred because I have known and loved so many brothers in Christ in Japan who have been hung. With my Quaker background, I find it difficult to see how Christians can continue to live by the Old Testament rule of "an eye for an eye and a tooth for a tooth." Christ forgave the murderer on the cross and said to the woman who had committed adultery, "Neither do I condemn thee. Go and sin no more." Modern prisons should be for rehabilitation, not for vengeance.

Our last four years in Japan were spent in Mito living in a tiny Japanese house owned by the Friends' Mission. I was head of the *yoroen* (old folks' home) which we changed to *Aiyuen* (Love, Friendship Garden). I helped Susumu Yamaguchi in his work on the buildings so they would be fireproof and in creating a Christian spirit in the home. We spent many hours at the provincial welfare office, at the welfare office in Tokyo, and at the Community Chest, trying to get funds for rebuilding.

We also went to local banks, companies, and individuals for contributions. Very little money for this work came from America. Local Japanese Rotary Clubs became interested in our project, so I was frequently asked to speak to various groups, especially at Christmastime. Each year we received funds for building a new section or two until we had a splendid concrete building with room for about 80 guests.

Every year on the Emperor's birthday, it is traditional for the heads of various independent welfare institutions to be called to the governor's office to receive a gift from the Emperor. It is quite a formal affair. All stand before the governor while he makes a speech and presents us each with an envelope. Then one of us is expected to step forward to make a speech of thanks for the whole group.

The last time I appeared at such a gathering, I was urged to make the speech. I protested, saying that I really did not know the proper language for such a formal occasion. I suggested, instead, that the oldest person present should make the speech. Everyone agreed. I had made the suggestion because there was an obviously ancient gentleman standing next to me who I figured must surely be older than I. But, when we compared ages, I discovered to my dismay that I was two years older than he was! Everybody laughed and clapped their hands, so I had no choice but to do the best I could.

I stepped forward, when the time came, and made a speech of acceptance and gratitude in my very best Japanese. Then on an impulse, I was very, very rude. I knew that the lovely envelope I had been given contained but one crisp thousand *yen* bill (about $3. at that time), so I remarked—very politely, of course—what a burden it put on us to decide what to do with this small amount of money without being disrespectful to His Majesty the Emperor. Fortunately, the governor enjoyed the joke and laughed heartily.

When New Year's approached, I was called to the governor's office again. This time he told me that our *Aiyuen* had been chosen as one of ten institutions in the whole nation to receive a New Year's present from Emperor Hirohito of 30,000 yen, nearly $100. I accepted the gift with gradatude.

Our days remained busy, as always. We continued visiting hospitals, leprosaria, and prisons. Nearly every day Madeline and I walked over to the national hospital in Mito where the children's ward was a special joy to us. But then in January, 1959, we had word from the Mukti Mission in India that our daughter, Virginia, was not well, and that a visit from her mother might help.

Madeline needed to leave immediately in order to arrive in India before the hot season began. We heard the news on a Saturday, and the next Tuesday Madeline was in Bombay! She was the first missionary mother to visit the mission. The missionaries there, the women and girls at the mission, all received her with much love. The little ones called her *Ahji* (grandma), and loved to jabber to her in Marathi, thinking she understood what they said. Perhaps she did! There are some things that know no language barriers. After three months Virginia was well again, so Madeline returned to Japan.

In 1957 our son Samuel married Anna Margaret Atkinsonin a Quaker ceremony in Pennsylvania. During the hot season of 1960 Virginia came to Mito for a vacation. While she was there we persuaded Madeline to fly to America to attend the wedding of our son Donald to Mildred Purdy. My brother Paul performed the ceremony and Samuel was the best man. A tape recording was made of the wedding so that Virginia and I could hear it.

After the wedding our son Samuel came again to Japan with his wife, and their young son, Peter. They had been appointed to work with the Japan Committee of the Philadelphia Yearly Meeting. Samuel had become interested in pottery, so when he arrived he started a pottery project at *Aiyuen*. This has developed into a real industry. The people there also raise flowers and have opportunities to go outside for work. This makes the *Aiyuen* quite popular, and it is always full.

In October of 1960, I hosted a tour party from Honolulu led by Reverend Paul Nagano. I had arranged a 25-day tour of Christian institutions in Japan for $10 a day. It was a good price at that time, as the tourist bureau charged double that amount. I made all the arrangements and met the chartered plane carrying 61 people when they arrived in Tokyo.

We spent 25 wonderful days together, travelling all over Japan visiting hospitals, missions, children's homes, churches, schools, and many things no regular tourist to Japan would be likely to see. Everywhere we went we were received most hospitably by both the Japanese and the missionaries. The experience was truly memorable.

When it was all over, there was $2,000 left from the tour. This was given to Madeline and me as a gift. We used half of it to make contributions to some of the institutions we had visited. The balance we used for a tour of the Orient to try to find places where Japanese missionaries could work. Besides, Madeline had had such a wonderful visit to India that I wanted to visit there, too!

We knew that our days in our beloved adopted country were numbered. In my seventieth year, 1961, we decided that we had better return to Pasadena. We had been in Japan a total of 35 years. Leaving again was a difficult decision to make.

Before we could depart, we wanted to spend one more summer at Karuizawa. How we loved our little cottage and all our friends there! We sold the cottage that summer and divided the money with our children.

As the time approached for us to leave, there were farewell meetings in many places, leprosaria, hospitals, churches, prisons. The Christian governor of Ibaraki Ken invited us to dinner and gave us a letter of appreciation that I especially treasure. He wrote:

> *When you arrived in Mito you were very*
> *young, and it was in those days, a rare sight to see*
> *you dashingly go by on your bicycle. You are*
> *now leaving us, and your hair turns gray a little.*
> *We find it very difficult to say good-bye to you as*
> *we are filled up with your kindness.*
>
> *I would like to make special mention of the one*
> *thing that we are very hard to forget, and that is*
> *that during the war while you were in the States,*
> *you extended your warm, helping hands without*
> *regarding your own personal danger for*
> *Japanese internees. Then after the war you came*
> *to ruined Japan with LARA goats and the other*
> *relief goods to keep off our hunger. These noble*
> *undertakings of yours are so near and dear to our*
> *souls that we shall not easily let them slip from our*
> *memories. They will surely become a bridge of*
> *good will between Japan and America.*
>
> *"God speed you" in good measure.*
>
> *With highest respect,*
>
> *Niro Iwakami*
> *Governor of Ibaraki Prefecture*

After a final farewell at the Tokyo Friends' Meeting, we were finally off for Yokohama where we boarded our steamer. As we left the harbor, both Madeline and I felt in our hearts that this was our last sailing from our beloved Japan. We did return to Japan briefly, however, in 1963 when Dr. Okouchi and Dr. Tokita treated Madeline's arthritis. Her condition improved a great deal and we had a wonderful visit with Samuel and Anna Margaret and our two grandsons, Peter and six-month-old Christopher.

Chapter 19

Home But Not Retired

The 20 years that have passed since we returned to Pasadena have been active ones. When we arrived home in California, Madeline and I felt we were not retired, just "re-tread," ready for further service. Before long we were busy visiting the sick and elderly, and helping with services in Japanese churches.

In the summer of 1972 we were officially put on the staff of JEMS (Japanese Evangelistic Missionary Society) as hospital chaplains. The Japanese Church Federation also asked us to serve in caring for their senior citizens. Every week we drove about Los Angeles visiting several hundred sick folks in hospitals and in nursing homes. On my 81st birthday, I was given a driver's license for four more years. On my 85th birthday, it was renewed again for four more!

Even at our advanced age, new things happened to us. For example, during these busy years I became an author.

About 1965, Mrs. Anne Loftis called on me. She and Mrs. Audrie Girdner had been asked by The MacMillan Co. to compile a history of the evacuation. I had several hours of conference with her, giving her much material and the names of people I thought she should see. *The Great Betrayal,* their impressive documentary account, was published in 1969. I was very excited about everything that came into print describing what the Japanese had suffered, but I never thought I would write a book myself.

In March of 1970, the Japanese American Church Federation of Southern California gave a banquet to honor us on the occasion of our golden wedding anniversary. The large social hall of the Los Angeles Free Methodist Church overflowed with more than 400 guests. What a time we had! There were speeches, songs, hymns, gifts, and prayers. 97-year-old Mrs. Kay Hiraiwa placed "leis" of golden folded paper storks about our necks. Rev. George Toda, with his rich, melodious voice sang, "To God be the Glory, Great Things He Hath Done," while we all joined in the chorus, "Praise the Lord, Praise the Lord." It was one of the most wonderful experiences of our lives.

Rev. Frank Omi wrote up our life story for publication in the large Los Angeles Japanese newspaper, *Rafu Shimpo.* It ran for five days preceding the banquet. After reading our story in the paper, many Japanese encouraged me to write down all our experiences in book form, so I decided to try. However, when I put pen to paper, my stories seemed to lose life.

I wrote about the problem to my friend Dorothy Clark Wilson, whose missionary biographies I had been selling for years. I asked if she would consider writing our life story for us. She suggested, instead, that when I sat down at my typewriter I should write as if I were talking to someone. I did just that, and with the help of friends, got out a little book for Christmas, 1972, called *Treasure in Earthen Vessels.* Originally the book was not for sale. We had 2,500 copies printed and sent most of them out as our Christmas message for the year.

The response was wonderful. People wrote to us sending

gifts and asking for more copies. By March all our copies were gone and the entire printing was paid for with $1,000 left over.

Many of our friends had suggested that the book should be translated into Japanese, so I decided to use the extra $1,000 to see if it could be done. For help I turned to my friend, Bob Gerry, of Christian Literature Crusade in Tokyo. Though I knew it might not be possible, I wanted Bob to see if Kaoru Kohama could do the translation. I knew Kohama was much in demand for translation projects, so I was frankly amazed and very pleased when I heard that he had agreed to do it. It was printed in 1974 under the title *Uncle Goat,* an expression taken from the days when I had brought goats for relief to Japan after the war.

The publication of our story in English and Japanese has brought us many interesting experiences and some new friends. One day while I was cutting my lawn, a gentleman came into the yard, took off his coat and finished the job for me! I invited him into the house and he told me that he was Rev. Yoji Sato of the Covina Japanese Community Church. The day before, he had been in Little Tokyo and bought a copy of my book *Yagi no Ojisan* (Uncle Goat). He kept reading until he had finished it, at four in the morning. He said that the Holy Spirit cleansed him from head to foot, and he felt he must go visit "Uncle Goat" right away. We had two hours of warm Christian fellowship.

Madeline and I have always worked together. When we were first married we lived with an elderly Japanese teacher who wrote our name in Chinese characters *Ni Ko Ru Son,* which might be translated as "God's sunshine came in to stay." There have been cloudy days with heartbreaks, but thanks to God, His sunshine has always come through the clouds. Our rule has always been never to "let the sun go down" on our wrath. And what a wonderful life Madeline and I have had together. It's hard to believe that 61 years have sped by since we were married in Kyoto in 1920.

For many years Madeline experienced pain from a calci-fied hip which she fractured in 1960. She began using a cane, then crutches, a walker, and finally a wheel chair. As long as we could, Virginia and I got her up every day and she went with me to visit the sick and attend church services. At one point retired orthopedic surgeon Dr. Joseph Risser, an old friend, suggested an operation to replace her hip and ease the pain, but he was overruled by a younger doctor who felt Madeline would not be able to rehabilitate at her age. So Dr. Risser said kindly, "Madeline, you'll just have to grin and bear it."

With a flash of her old wit Madeline replied, "Herbie will do the grinning and I'll do the bearing!" God bless her!

On our 57th wedding anniversary, March 31, 1977, Madeline became ill and had to be hospitalized. Ulcers were suspected, but X-rays showed nothing. The pain medication she had been taking for her hip was probably the cause of her symptoms.

The three-day hospital stay put additional strain on Madeline's already somewhat confused state of mind. While there she kept calling for me continuously, and so had to be sedated. The combined effect of the sedation and the disorientation she experienced being in a strange place taxed her fading memory to the fullest. When she was brought home, we found that her mind had completely dimmed. She has slept peacefully day and night since that time, waking only occasionally to say a few words to us. Fortunately she no longer feels any pain. How happy I am that she has not had to be taken away, and Virginia and I can care for her in our own home.

After the publication of my book in Japanese, Bob Gerry in Tokyo began encouraging me to consider making a trip to Japan. I would have lots of opportunities to speak in mission schools and in churches. I could also help Christian

Literature Crusade sell the Japanese edition of my book. I was thrilled to think about seeing Japan once again. On my 83rd birthday, January 30, 1975, I was booked to fly. Madeline, of course, could not go with me, although she was not yet completely bedridden at that time.

Then, a slight warning caused me to go to the doctor. I was found to have a malignancy of the colon. On January 23, just one week before my scheduled trip for Japan, I had surgery. The trip was off.

The cancer was caught in time and my recovery was good. Before too long I was able to resume my regular life visiting sick elderly Japanese, going to churches, and looking after my Madeline. However, it looked like my opportunity to go to Japan was gone.

In December of 1977, I received a letter from Michi Weglyn whose book, *Years of Infamy*, about the Japanese in America during World War II, I had been promoting. Michi's father had been in one of the nursing homes I visited every week. During the last months before his death of cancer, Michi and her husband, Walter, came from New York to be with him. I often saw them and we became friends.

Michi knew of my interest in anything to promote the cause of peace, so she wrote me about a friend of hers, Dennis Roland. Dennis had been a prisoner of war under the Japanese in Burma. At his own expense he had returned there, and, as a demonstration of forgiveness, had walked across the bridge over the river Kwai with his arms around his former prison guards. Now as an expression of sympathy he wanted to go to Japan for the memorial meetings which are held in remembrance of the many who died in the atomic bombings of Hiroshima and Nagasaki.

This appealed to me as a wonderful gesture of good will, so I put a note in our annual Christmas letter, asking for financial support for this project. By January I had received enough to send two people. I wrote Dennis asking if he knew of any other former prisoner of war who might like to go. Dennis contacted R. Ernest Gordon, chaplain of Princeton University chapel. Dr. Gordon, who had also been a prisoner of war in Burma, agreed to go.

It was important for whoever went to the memorial meetings to take a gift for the survivors of the atomic bombs. Michi consulted Paul Tsuneishi of the Pacific Southwest Council of the Japanese American Citizens League. He suggested that the JACL might sponsor a "recognition" dinner for Madeline and me which might serve as a fund raiser for the project.

Harry Honda of the *Pacific Citizen* offered to assist in the marketing of a book about Madeline's and my involvement with the evacuated Japanese during World War II. Profits from the book would be added to the fund. Betty Mitson, director of the Japanese American Oral HIstory Project at California State University, Fullerton, agreed to work with Michi co-editing a publication of some of Betty's interviews with me and excerpts from my book, *Treasure in Earthen Vessels.*

Producing the small book was a nerve-wracking process for all of us. But when the final product, *Valiant Odyssey,* came out it was a great success. Most of the 2,500 copies were sold in a month and by June we had $5,000, the equivalent of a million *Yen* at that time, for Hiroshima.

As if this were not enough for an old man, when I heard that Japanese were trying to get 35 million signatures on a petition against nuclear weapons for the special disarmament session at the United Nations, I felt that the Japanese in America might like to join in. I had petitions printed in Japanese and English and sent them to all Japanese churches, many Buddhist temples, Friend's meetings, and to some churches of Mennonites and Brethren as well. As most were sent directly to the United Nations, I do not know how many petitions were actually sent in, but there must have been many.

Then Dr. Gordon wrote that he could not go with Dennis to Japan. Virginia, my daughter urged me to go in his place, offering to combine vacation time from her nursing job at Keiro Home with additional time off at her own expense in order to take care of Madeline while I would be away. She knew how much I wanted to go.

Knowing Madeline would be in loving hands I felt I could go. I was booked on a 26-day Japanese American Citizen's League tour flight leaving Los Angeles July 25, 1978. And so my 86th year turned out to be one of the best years of my life!

Just two days before I left, July 23, thanks to Paul Tsuneishi's efforts, eight different Japanese organizations sponsored an "Evening with Reverend and Mrs. Herbert V. Nicholson." Virginia went with me to represent her mother and the whole evening was marvelous. When my turn to say something came, I poured out my heart in English and Japanese for over half an hour. What overflowing love was showered on us that night! Many have told us it was one of the most wonderful occasions they had ever attended.

When I got home I emptied my pockets and found over $1,000 in checks and cash had been slipped to me by loving friends. The Japanese American Citizen's League office received over $4,000, which meant that I had another million *Yen* for Nagasaki.

The 26 days I spent in Japan were the most wonderful days of my whole life.

On August 6, 1978, I was at Hiroshima with Dennis to lay flowers on the memorial cenataph, visit the Governor and Mayor, and attend the large memorial meeting. I visited a large hospital and home for the aged and presented copies of my Japanese book, *Yagi no Ojisan* (Uncle Goat), to several A-bomb sufferers. On August 9, we were at Nagasaki to visit the Mayor, a large hospital, Catholic old folk's home, and the memorial meeting.

I made many stops and visited countless friends on the way back to Tokyo and acted as father to Kitty Taylor when she married Takashi Mizuno at the Tokyo Friends Meeting. Sunday, August 20, I attended meetings in Tsuchiura, Mito, and Shomotsuma, getting back to Tokyo near midnight. After a refreshing night's sleep, I was ready to go on Fujii television at 8 a.m. for a popular show with my old friend Ryumei Yamano. It was wonderful to have a chance to bid millions of Japanese people a fond farewell.

Throughout my stay Japanese Friends graciously paid all my expenses. The love, gifts, and care that were lavished on me by so many, friends and strangers, was heartwarming.

When I got home, Madeline spoke to me, but did not realize that I had been gone. I began at once going about giving reports of my trip to a different Japanese church each Sunday. It was a most wonderful time. Everywhere I spoke the people responded warmly.

In September of 1979 I had another slight warning that I should see my doctor. A barium X-ray revealed another tumor right at the rectum. Various tests showed that it was malignant, but very local. I needed surgery again.

The surgeon was reluctant to operate on me because of my age. I was 87. The chances were one in ten that I wouldn't pull through. This brought tears to my eyes and I said, "But I don't want to go and leave Madeline on Virginia's hands."

After a moment I asked the surgeon, "Are you a Christian?"

"I am a Methodist," he replied.

I explained that being a Methodist did not necessarily make him a Christian. "Do you know how to pray?"

"I guess so," he faltered.

"There is to be no guesswork about it," I declared. "We are going to have to have prayer!"

I immediately sent messages to Japan asking friends and loved ones to pray for me. I had also phoned Japanese churches asking for prayer. Within a few days I had many assurances of prayer from friends both in Japan and here at home, so I entered the hospital unafraid.

Surgery was scheduled for early Monday morning, September 24. When I regained consciousness afterward, I discovered that I was back in my hospital room, not in intensive care as I'd expected. Jumping to the conclusion that for some reason the doctors had been unable to operate, I asked what happened. Just then my surgeon came in beaming. "It's all over," he said. "You came through like a teenager! No transfusions, no intensive care. Somebody must have prayed!"

Because of the tumor's location, it had not been removed. Instead I had a colostomy and was given six weeks of radiation treatment. This worked wonderfully well. The cancer was gone and the colostomy worked beautifully. The doctors said I should have several more years to serve the Lord and care for Madeline.

When I got home from the hospital Madeline welcomed me by waking up to say that she loved me VERY MUCH. Then she slipped back into peaceful sleep without pain. Virginia works only two nights a week now in order to have more time to care for us and some other sick friends.

In summer, 1981, the day after I left the hospital from my third bout with cancer, I gave my witness at the Los Angeles hearings of the Congressional Commission on Redress to Evacuated Japanese. I got a big hand when I started out by saying that the government should have paid in full all that was asked for in 1948 instead of only 10%. There was no other Caucasian more involved in the tragic evacuation than I. I suffered with my church people. I followed the Issei who were rounded up like common criminals and taken to Missoula, then to prisoners-of-war camps after mock trials!

When I went to relocation centers, I ate and slept with the internees, suffering the heat and dust storms of Arizona and the cold of Heart Mountain. I even spent one night in a filthy jail in Colorado and was continually hounded by the FBI. So I was sympathetic with all the sad experiences.

Our government needs to make financial restitution that would be symbolic of the fact that the evacuation in 1942 was an unconstitutional action. There are various opinions about the best way in which financial restitution might be made. I have urged my Issei and Nisei friends to express their own opinions by letter to the Congressional Commission. I have corresponded with several of the commission members myself, all of whom have expressed appreciation for my testimony. Judge William Marutani, a Nisei who chaired the hearing, has written that my words were "a refreshing interlude, quite different from much they had been receiving."

I am happy for every opportunity I have had over the years to work for the cause of peace. Madeline and I are not ashamed to be known as Friends, for like George Fox, the founder of Quakerism, we have found that there is "One, Christ Jesus, who can speak to our condition." Many of our dearest friends do not agree with some of our Friendly convictions. We stand for a spiritual experience that will help us live the good life, and that is at the heart of all committed Christians. Only at the fringes of our various denominations do differences occur.

We believe the tide will turn—the death penalty will eventually be outlawed, and Christian conscientious objection to war will be embraced. When Christ told his disciples to love as he loved, it included loving their enemies! Of course, that is very difficult. It can be accomplished only as we are filled with the Spirit of Christ.

Now is the time to lay down my pen. Dear Madeline is 93 and I'll be 90 before this book is read. It has been such a joy reliving our life together that I hate to stop! But the end is not yet. As long as we live, the story will continue to unfold.

Herbert V. Nicholson
1639 Locust Street
Pasadena, California 91106

Appendix

BIBLIOGRAPHY

BOOKS

Bacon, Margaret H. *The Quiet Rebels: the Story of the Quakers in America.* Basic Books, Inc. New York, 1969, 229 pp.

Girdner, Audrie and Anne Loftis. *The Great Betrayal: the Evacuation of the Japanese during World War II.* The MacMillan Company, London, 1969, 562 pp.

Hansen, Arthur A. and Betty E. Mitson, eds. *Voices Long Silent: An Inquiry into the Japanese American Evacuation.* California State University, Fullerton Japanese American Project, 1974, 216 pp.

Hasakawa, Bill. *Nisei: The Quiet Americans.* Wm. Morrow and Company, Inc. New York, 1969, 522 pp.

Kitagawa, Daisuke. *Issei and Nisei: the Internment Years.* The Seabury Press, New York, 1967, 174 pp.

Lord, Walter, *Day of Infamy.* Bantam Books. Hart, Rinehart and Winston, Inc. New York, 1970, 245 pp.

Mitson, Betty E. and Michi Weglyn, eds. *Valiant Odyssey: Herbert Nicholson in and out of America's Concentration Camps.* Brunk's Printing, Upland, California, 1978, 78 pp.

Myer, Dillon S. *Uprooted Americans: the Japanese Americans and the War Relocation during World War II.* The University of Arizona Press, Tucson, Arizona, 1971, 360 pp.

Nicholson, Herbert V. *Japan Diary 1978: Overflowing Love.* Brunk's Printing, Upland, California, 1979.

Nicholson, Herbert V. *Treasure in Earthen Vessels: God's Love Overflows in Peace and War.* Penn Lithographics, Inc. Whittier, California, 1974, 152 pp.

TAPES

Herbert V. Nicholson, interviewed in Pasadena, California, April 19 and 24, July 19, and November 20, 1973 by Betty E. Mitson, then Director of the Japanese American Oral History Project at California State University at Fullerton.

Excerpt from Magazine Article —
"Empty the Relocation Centers"

The experience of one of my friends is impressive. Herbert Nicholson, after twenty-five years of missionary service in Japan with the Quakers, is now running a free trucking service in and out of Los Angeles to the Manzanar, Poston and Gila River centers. He does every conceivable type of shopping and errand-running for many of the 35,000 residents of these centers, and has everything from pianos to canary birds. On one return trip he carried with him for burial, the ashes of a friend's beloved son. He is entrusted with keys to safety deposit vaults and is sometimes authorized to sign valuable papers. He visits sick relatives in Los Angeles hospitals. Twice he has made long tours of concentration camps, bringing and taking messages for husbands and sons behind the barbed wire.

I rode with him from Pasadena into Poston and Gila River, with a box of cut flowers and three dogs on top of the load. The appearance of his truck in camp was greeted like the arrival of Santa Claus. Truly he is a glorified messenger boy! And for this manifold service he makes no charge whatever. But his efforts are so appreciated that he is constantly in peril of being overpaid. A dozen times I heard him arguing with friends that the amounts offered were excessive, and saw him handing back a substantial proportion of the sums offered. He no longer dares to accept a sealed envelope: it will surely contain twice as much as the proper amount for transportation costs.

Page, Kirby, "Empty the Relocation Centers," *The Christian Century*, pp. 715-716, June 1943

MID 201,
NICHOLSON, Herbert (H.V.)

WAR DEPARTMENT
M. I. D.
Washington 25

<u>24 August 1943</u>
(Date)

Subject: <u>NICHOLSON</u>, Herbert (H.V.)
1554 Las Lunas Street
Pasadena, California
Summary of Information:

According to an article appearing in the Rafu Shimpo, Los Angeles bi-lingual Japanese daily on 22 January 1942, the Rev. and Mrs. Herbert (H.V.) NICHOLSON are particularly prominent members of a committee in charge of "aid to distressed resident Japanese families".

The above committee is one of a number of committees of the AMERICAN FRIENDS SERVICE COMMITTEE which is affiliated with the AMERICAN QUAKER GROUP. Although there is no indication of subversive intent on the part of this committee , which has been under investigation by the Federal Bureau of Investigation, it appears that its interracial and international connections leave it liable to manipulation by anti-American elements.

In its Sunday edition of 28 March 1943, the Des Moines Register-Tribune, on the "People's Open Forum" page devoted about two and a half columns of space to several articles favoring more equitable treatment of loyal Japanese. A "letter to the editor" occupying a large share of this space was written by H. V. NICHOLSON, 1554 Las Lunas Street, Pasadena, California. "Letters to the Editor" were under the main caption: "Nisei Ideals Declared as High as any Person's— One Contributor Thinks Democratic and Christian America Should Set Example for the world". A photograph allegedly showing the evacuation from the West Coast was printed on the page with this caption: ".... this wholesale evacuation from the West Coast was primarily caused by certain high pressure economic and political groups using false propaganda about sabotage in Hawaii to influence the primitive minds of the American people. These false stories have been officially denied but the damage was done," a quotation from the NICHOLSON letter.

Previous Distribution:
ONI
7SC

Distribution:
Assistant Secretary of War

Evaluation
-of source / -of information
Reliable
Credible
Questionable
Undetermined
C   3

-CONFIDENTIAL-

```
Facsimile of Document from
National Archives, Record
Group 210, Entry 19.  Origi-
nally "Classified;" declass-
ified, Dept. of Interior letter
of Dec. 1, 1965, per NCAS-JFS



                    WAR RELOCATION AUTHORITY
                    San Francisco 5, California


                                        (No typed date,
                                        stamped Oct. 7, 1944)


        Mr. Dillon S. Myer
        Director
        War Relocation Authority
        Barr Building
        Washington 25, D.C.

        Dear Mr. Myer:

            Enclosed is a copy of excerpts from a sermon made by
        Reverend Nicholson at Gila on July 3 which is, I believe,
        concurred in by both Tom Sawyer and Mr. Johnson of the
        Washington Office.

            I am wondering if we should let this go by or if
        we should discuss this not only with Mr. Nicholson but
        also with those to whom he is somewhat responsible in
        Southern California.  Also, I wonder if you want to give
        this to other projects that he visits.

            As you know, Mr. Nicholson has been talking here
        on the West Coast for sometime and has kept us in hot
        water.

            I am not doing anything with this but giving it
        to you for information.

                                    Sincerely,



                                    R. B. Cozzens
                                    Assistant Director


        Enclosure
```

1554 Las Lunas St., Pasadena 4, Calif.
August 11, 1945

Hon. John J. McCloy
Asst. Secretary of War
Pentagon Bldg.
Washington D. C.

Dear Mr. McCloy: -

In March 1944 I was in your office protesting against indiscriminate bombing of our enemies. At that time you assured me you would only bomb military objectives. Three months ago I again wrote in protest of the terrific bombing of residential areas of Japanese cities and I was again assured that no "unnecessary" harm would be done to civilians and that America would fight according to the Geneva Convention.

In the use of this diabolical atomic bomb any one with a sense of justice would say that America has certainly broken these assurances. I do not believe that you realize the general revulsion on the part of the public of this terrible thing. At a meeting of some twenty persons, preachers, social workers, etc., yesterday here in Pasadena every one was sure that their neighbors, the common man, was at last stirred up to see the terribleness of this awful thing. We feel positive that if the American people had been given all the facts and a chance to determine, that we would not have permitted this thing.

We hope and pray that peace might be granted now with the condition that the Emperor be allowed to reamin in power as a force for law and order in Japan. Surely, we are the greatest hypocrites possible if we say we are fighting for rights of people to determine their own destiny and then go in and tell them what they should do. In the end this whole dastardly thing will come back to us. We can only reap what we sow. The day of reckoning is surely coming for America.

I regret that I have to write in this strain, as you are in a very difficult position. You have stood for righteousness, but the hard-fisted militarist element in our army has won out and I am personally very sorry. Now is the time for the more liberal element to stand out against such extremes, knowing that you have the people of the United States behind you.

Very sincerely yours,

H. V. Nicholson

President H. S. Truman
The White House
Washington, D. C.

1554 Las Lunas St., Pasadena 4, Calif.
August 11, 1945

Dear Mr. President: -

On several occasions in the past I have protested against the indiscriminate bombing of enemy towns. Personally I see little difference in the wrong of killing people by the thousands or hundreds of thousands. However, I wish you could know the terrible revulsion towards this diabolic atomic bomb that has arisen amongst the common people of your country. I believe that if by a democratic process with the facts fairly presented to the people of the United States that we would have voted against this most uncivilized thing.

There are two very dangerous things that I would like to point out in this whole war system. First, you rely on the unChristian theory that the "end justifies the means." Second, we, who are also "war criminals" are in no position to judge others. In a court of justice the two parties involved are never named as judges. There must be a neutral judge. It is very evident that we are not going to get justice out of this fiasco. In the end - and even right now in our own consciences - there will be righteous judgment by a Just and Loving God.

It is perhaps too late already to influence in any way your decision about the answer to Japan's request for peace. Hundreds of thousands of loyal Americans are praying and hoping that you accept the terms in regard to the Emperor. I have lived in Japan for 25 years and am convinced that if we wish to make any kind of a peace with that country we must leave the Emperor on the throne. That is entirely a question for the people of Japan to fight out and decide for themselves.

I do not wish to be critical, as I know that you have been thrust into a most difficult position; but my heart does long for justice and the ways of peace.

Very sincerely yours,

H. V. Nicholson

Madeline thought my letter to President Truman was too strong, so she wrote the following to send instead.

President H. S. Truman
The White House
Washington, D. C.

1554 Las Lunas St., Pasadena 4, Calif.
August 11, 1945

Dear Mr. President: -

Our hearts go out to you in this time of tremendous responsibility, which has been thrust upon you. The people of the United States have been, on the whole, encouraged in the way you have handled the difficult situations which you have had to meet. We believe that God will answer your appeal for help and guidance, given in such a truly Christian, humble spirit - for God alone can bring peace and order out of chaos.

I feel strongly that if you understood the situation in Japan you would agree to leaving the Emperor in Japan as the symbol he is. The warring factors in old Japan were brought together under the Emperor as a symbol - he himself has no real power. If he were removed, the symbol of law and order would be destroyed, not only for that nation, but for those who try to keep order in that country, it would leave an almost hopeless situation.

The real power there has been in the advisers of the Emperor, now being the military leaders. If the right advisers and counselors were used the work could be done infinitely better, by the retention of the Emperor.

The love and confidence of the people of the United States is with you, and we pray, with you, that God may guide you into right decisions -and may give you health and strength to carry on through these difficult times.

Very sincerely,

(Mrs. H. V.) Madeline V. Nicholson

NUCLEAR WEAPONS — NO!

We have raised enough money to send Dennis Roland, a former prisoner of the Japanese (survivor of the Burma/Thai death railway and the River Kwai Bridge), to Hiroshima and Nagasaki next August to beg forgiveness of A-bomb sufferers in the name of the American people. We are now raising money for him to take as a gift to them.

Dennis has totally dedicated his life to the on-going peoples' drive to ban forever nuclear warfare. In Japan, the forces of peace have united in an effort to try to get thirty-five million signatures on a petition they are taking to the United Nations Disarmament Congress next June. In America, peace-loving people are also uniting to get many more millions of signatures: and a great mass meeting is being planned for the Hollywood Bowl May 21st — just before the Disarmament Congress meets in New York.

It is my concern that those of Japanese ancestry in this country take part in the campaign. I would like to see 100,000 of us sign such petitions. These petitions are now being printed and I am hoping to receive copies momentarily. In the meanwhile, I am trying to get various Nikkei organizations to begin making preparations to participate in this momentous international effort.

It is high time that the peoples of the world rise up and demand that something effective be done about this dire, unnecessary menace to mankind. Time is running out. Pressure must be brought on the United Nations, all heads of state, and those in positions of power throughout the world.

I am also concerned about the A-bomb survivors (Hibakushas) in our midst as well as in Japan. Many of them are still suffering terribly. More medical help is needed than is provided by their respective governments. The Committee of Atomic Bomb Survivors in the United States of America (1109 Shell Gate Place, Alameda, Ca. 93401) desperately needs our attention, sympathy and help. They report that two bills are now before the House in regard to this: HR 5150 and HR 8440. I hope you will write your Representatives and Senators on this subject. Here again, let us rise up and demand that something concrete be done for these suffering people.

I am continuing in my efforts to raise a sizable gift of money for Dennis Roland to take to this group (in Alameda), and also to Hiroshima and Nagasaki, as a token of our sympathy. It would make me very happy to hear from any of you who might wish to help.

Herbert V. Nicholson
1639 Locust Street
Pasadena, California 91106
(213) 792-8944   1981

L.A. Redress Hearings Concluded
Community Stands Behind Monetary Compensation

The Federal Commission on Wartime Relocation and Internment of Civilians ended three days of hearings in Los Angeles Thursday evening. In all, more than 200 witnesses gave testimony before the presidentially and congressionally-nominated panel, which is charged with reviewing the facts and circumstances surrounding Executive Order 9066 and the impact of the order on American citizens and permanent resident aliens and to recommend appropriate remedies.

One of the highlights of the Thursday testimony was a statement by long-time civil liberties attorney Fred Okrand, of the American Civil Liberties Union.

Okrand, speaking as part of a panel on constitutional issues involved in the World War II evacuation and incarceration of Japanese America, called the Supreme Court's decision in the landmark **Korematsu v. United States,** which deemed the evacuation constitutional, "wrong" and characterized the high court's decision as "a judicial precedent which fed upon expediency."

The legendary ACLU counsel went on to say the U.S. actions against Nikkei during WWII had a "melancholy resemblance to what was done in Nazi Germany."

"The idea of monetary compensation is correct," Okrand told the commission. "Little will have been accomplished here without compensation—we could have all stayed home."

He added that monetary compensation is historically provided for as reparations for wrongful incarceration. The imprisonment of Japanese Americans, he offered, was a "colossally large wrongful incarceration."

On the same panel, Rose Matsui Ochi, a legislative planner for Mayor Tom Bradley, said the incarceration was a "castration of the Japanese American psyche." She added it was "ludicrous to ask if a wrong was committed," saying a failure of the U.S. government to provide compensation would represent a second betrayal of Japanese in America.

A friendly voice out of the past, the Rev. Herbert V. Nicholson of Pasadena, came from a hospital bed to testify on behalf of the Nikkei redress movement.

Nicholson, 88, who assisted the Nikkei community before, during and after their wartime ordeal, advocated the foundaton of a memorial fund for those who perished during their imprisonment in concentration camps for Japanese Americans. He suggested that the U.S. government should start by appropriating "several million dollars" for such a fund.

He also suggested that the government help pay for the Japanese American Cultural Community Center in Los Angeles and publicize the loyalties of the Japanese Americans during WWII.

Nicholson left the hearing room to loud applause from the 300 in attendance.

Other key testimonies during the L.A. hearings will be published in full in upcoming editions of **The Rafu Shimpo**.

A fitting close to the three historic days of testimony in Los Angeles was contained in a presentation by California State University, Long Beach researcher, Larry Boss. His study of Japanese American losses because of the WWII evacuation and imprisonment indicated that Nikkei lost more that $40 billion in land, residences, farms, retail business, personal property and wages.

Boss' study estimate of the Japanese American losses did not include possible damages for psychological damages and increases in land values.

Boss, the final witness to appear before the commission, testified that if the government were to recompense Japanese America for only the losses identified in his study, it would have to pay victims of the camps "a third of a million dollars each."

The L.A. hearings, which attracted turn-away crowds all three days, elicited gut-wrenching, emotional testimony from former Japanese American camp inmates from throughout Southern California and, according to community organizers, lent added impetus to the current drives to gain reparations from the government for the injustices meted to Japanese America.

Testimony delivered at the hearings seemed to render questions of whether a wrong was committed against Japanese in America during World War II academic. However, commissioners present for the L.A. hearings, save for former Supreme Court Justice Arthur J. Goldberg, were reluctant to openly support a recommendation for redress and reparations.

The CWRIC will be holding hearings in San Francisco next week, in Seattle, Alaska and Chicago next month.

The commission is expected to deliver its report and recommendations to Congress next spring.

Dwight Chuman, Editor
The Rafu Shimpo
Los Angeles Japanese Daily News
August 17, 1981   Reprinted by permission

**COMMISSION ON WARTIME RELOCATION
AND INTERNMENT OF CIVILIANS**

726 JACKSON PLACE, N.W. □ SUITE 2020 □ WASHINGTON, D.C. 20506 □ 202/395-7390

August 12, 1981

Mr. Herbert Nicholson
1639 Locust Street
Pasadena, California 91106

Dear Mr. Nicholson:

Your letter of August 7, 1981 addressed to Joan Z.
Bernstein was referred to me for reply.

I appreciate very much your testimony at the Los Angeles
hearing. It was very nice to see you. We will also
include the supplement to your testimony in the
Commission's permanent record. Thank you for sending this
additional information to us.

Sincerely,

Paul T. Bannai
Executive Director

PTB:tw

WILLIAM M. MARUTANI
PHILADELPHIA, PENNSYLVANIA

17 August 1981

Herbert V. Nicholson
Pasadena

Dear Mr. Nicholson:

Thank you for your letter. Indeed, those Nisei who are opposed
to redress should appear and testify. It is important that
the Commission receive all viewpoints, particularly those who
are involved in the ultimate issue.

Insofar as "hard feelings," such unfortunately is an inescapable
consequence. There are yet all-too-many fellow citizens who
look upon persons who are not of the same race as non-Americans.
This view, of course, is un-American.

I was in Pinedale and then in Tule Lake, the latter for about
three months. I left the camps in October, 1942, to return to
school.

Indeed, I shall be reading the book you so kindly gave. I am
collecting all these books so that my offspring will have a
small library on the subject of this entire unfortunate episode
in our American history.

God Bless,

Bill M.

United States Commission on Civil Rights
Washington, D.C. 20425

Chairman

August 25, 1981

Reverend Herbert V. Nicholson
1639 Locust Street
Pasadena, California 91106

Dear Reverend Nicholson:

I appreciated so much receiving your cordial note of August 7.
I was indeed grateful for your testimony. It was very helpful.

Prior to your appearance as a witness, a number of other
witnesses had spoken in very appreciative terms of your ministry
in their behalf. As a lifelong Methodist and as a former President of the National Council of Churches, I want to express my
gratitude to you for the example that you have set for all of us.
Many Issei and Nissei, as well as many others who are deeply
concerned about the actions taken by our nation, are deeply
indebted to you.

Very best wishes.

                              Very sincerely and cordially yours,

                              ARTHUR S. FLEMMING

Reprinted by Permission

Index